# BEGINNER'S SPANISH

# BEGINNER'S SPANISH

ILA WARNER

HIPPOCRENE BOOKS
*New York*

For information, address:
HIPPOCRENE BOOKS, INC.
171 Madison Avenue
New York, NY 10016

ISBN 0-7818-0840-5

Printed in the United States of America.

# ACKNOWLEDGEMENTS

Even a modest book rarely gets written without the help of a good number of people. That was certainly true of this one.

Among those who contributed to the authenticity of the dialogues and cultural sections were helpful people in the embassies of Bolivia, the Dominican Republic, Chile, Peru, Panama and Nicaragua; the Columbian Coffee Federation; and Budget Rent-a-Car of Central America.

Individuals who merit special thanks are M. Booth Gathings, professor of Spanish and connoisseur of coffee; Nancy Gann, a native of Mexico, for help in all things Mexican; and Thomas Long, Salvadoran-based reporter for *The Economist* and other publications, for his information on motoring in Central America.

Also to be thanked for their input are a series of personal friends—natives and travelers to or longtime residents of Latin America—who are, unfortunately, too numerous to list.

And last, but most certainly not least, thanks are in order for Juanita Flores, Yolanda Hotman, Gloria Connor and Dr. Gerald Davey for "crisis intervention" with the author's accursed computer.

Ila Warner

# CONTENTS

# INTRODUCTION

Spanish is spoken in eighteen countries of the Western Hemisphere, making it the predominant language in that part of the world. And as the world shrinks—thanks to ever-expanding technology in such areas as transportation, communications and business—the ties between the English-speaking and Spanish-speaking world become stronger. There is, therefore, a pressing need to bridge the rather considerable gap between Anglo and Hispanic language and culture.

The aim of this book is to provide English speakers with a certain amount of basic instruction in the Spanish language together with highlights on certain linguistic differences between the various Latin American countries. Each lesson is dedicated to a Latin American country or region and includes a brief section on language differences important to English-speaking travelers.

As Spanish is spoken in so many of the countries of the Western Hemisphere, it is impossible to include even a brief outline of their histories, cultures and economic and political systems in the scope of this book. For this reason, this book focuses mostly on language, with details about its usage in the various Latin American countries.

No set pattern exists for the presentation of the grammatical structure of the Spanish language. Debates among language instructors as to the best sequence of structures to follow in teaching beginning language are about as resolvable as the one about how many angels can dance on the head of a pin. The simple fact, however, is that if one is to *master* a foreign language, he or she must ultimately absorb the entire body of the language's structure. This, of course, is not the aim of an introductory book. What you will find here are those structures most essential for basic communication.

# THE SPANISH OF LATIN AMERICA

Prior to the arrival of the Spanish *conquistadores* some 450 years ago, hundreds of Indian languages and dialects were spoken in the area of the Western Hemisphere that today we call Latin America. The principal Indian languages, spoken by numerous tribes of indigenous peoples, are Nahuatl, Maya, Quechua (or Quichua), Aymará and Guaraní. These languages are still spoken today by considerable numbers of the indigenous populations, Nahuatl in south central and coastal Mexico, Maya in the Yucatan, Quechua in the Andean regions, Aymará in Bolivia and Peru, and Guaraní principally in Paraguay.

In the time-honored manner of conquerors everywhere, the Spanish *conquistadores* lost no time in enslaving the Indians, then intermarried with them and imposed on them the religion, culture and language of their homeland.

However, the indigenous languages had their own impact on the Spanish language. For one thing, there existed in the New World a series of products and other objects that were completely unknown in Spain at that time, so quite logically the conquerors called them by their native names—*tabaco* (tabacco), *chile* (chili pepper), *hamacas* (hammocks) and so forth. Since the indigenous languages were often very different from one another, their impact on the Spanish language in the various parts of the hemisphere was different as well.

With the arrival of African slaves in the Caribbean, their languages had a certain limited influence on the Spanish of the region. Meanwhile, on the east coast of Central America you'll hear English, or a mixture of Spanish and English, as the result of a substantial immigration of West Indians from the English-speaking islands of the Caribbean.

In certain countries of South America, principally Chile and Argentina, a large proportion of their population is of European origin, especially German and Italian. These languages, too, have had their impact on the Spanish of that region. In Argentina for example, there is a type of slang known as Lunfardo that has been strongly influenced by Italian.

In most cases, the traveler to Latin America will not be in contact with people who speak the ancient Indian languages because these people most often live in remote rural areas. However, travelers will encounter words from their languages, as well as from a series of other language influences, on menus in restaurants, place-names on maps and labels on craft items in markets. And as the traveler crosses the border from one Latin American country to another, these words will likely change.

Consider this vast linguistic diversity an interesting challenge. Each lesson that follows in this book is dedicated to one country or region of Latin America and includes a few linguistic tips on usage as well as bits of cultural information that should be of practical use to travelers. Though brief, it is hoped that you will find them useful.

# SPANISH PRONUNCIATION

**B**ecause so many sounds in Spanish are similar to the English sound system, the pronunciation of Spanish is relatively easy. And (unlike English) the spelling and the pronunciation are very consistent. Spanish-speaking students of English always lament the fact that in English "you spell it one way and pronounce it another." English speakers learning Spanish are not faced with a similar problem.

An understanding of the following simple rules and a little practice should make it possible for English speakers to pronounce Spanish reasonably well. Here's how it goes:

## Consonants

The pronunciation of the majority of Spanish consonants is identical or very similar to their English counterparts. There are, of course, a few that have special characteristics. Below are explanations and/or examples of the sounds of all the Spanish consonants.

**b** and **v**     These consonants are pronounced alike depending on where they fall. At the beginning of a word both are pronounced like the **b** in "ball." Between vowels within a word they are pronounced like the **v** in "victory."

**c**     Sounds like **s** before **e** and **i**.
     Sounds like **k** before **a**, **o** and **u**.

| | |
|---|---|
| g | Sounds like the English **h** in "he" before **e** and **i**. Sounds like the **g** in "go" before **a**, **o** and **u**. |
| h | Always silent. |
| j | Like the English **h**. |
| ll | Like the **y** in "yes." |
| ñ | Like the **ny** in "canyon." |
| q | Always followed by **u** in Spanish and pronounced like the English **k**. |
| x | Before a consonant, like the English **s**; before a vowel, like "eggs." |
| z | Like the English **s**. |
| w and k | These are not a part of the Spanish alphabet, but they do appear in certain foreign words such as "karate" and "waffle." They are pronounced just as they are in the foreign words. |

## Vowels

The pronunciation of the vowels in Spanish is much easier than in English as they have only one sound apiece. English vowels can have as many as five to seven different sounds. But the very simplicity of the Spanish sound system sometimes trips up the English speaker. Accustomed as the English speaker is to the many nuances in the pronunciation of the English vowels, he or she is easily tempted to pronounce the first syllable in *casa* (house) like the first syllable in the English word "catch" and the final syllable like the "a" in the English word "father." That's why it's important to always bear in mind that each Spanish vowel has one and only one sound. These sounds are as follows:

| | |
|---|---|
| a | Like the **a** in "father." |
| e | Like the **a** in "way." |
| i | Like the first **e** in "even." |
| o | Like the **o** in "Oh!" |
| u | Like the **oo** in "tool." |

## Diphthongs

Combinations of a weak and a strong vowel or two weak vowels are called diphthongs. In Spanish, the strong vowels are **a**, **e** and **o**; the weak vowels, **i** and **u**.

The following are the more common diphthongs:

| | |
|---|---|
| **ai** | Sounds like **i** in "side." |
| **au** | Sounds like **ow** in "how." |
| **ei** | Sounds like **ay** in "stay." |
| **ia** | Sounds like **ya** in "yarn." |
| **ie** | Sounds like **ye** in "yellow." |
| **oi** | Sounds like **oy** in "toy." |

## Stress

In Spanish, if a word ends in a vowel, **n** or **s**, the stress naturally falls on the next-to-last syllable. If a word ends in a consonant other than **n** or **s**, the stress naturally falls on the final syllable.

If the pronunciation of a word differs from the above rules, the stressed syllable will be indicated with a written accent. Exception: Accents are usually not written over capital letters.

The above rules cover what is considered standard pronunciation. There are, of course, innumerable variations throughout the Spanish-speaking world. Consider first how many variations there are in the pronunciation of English. Compare the difference between British English and American English. Even within the United States there are many variations. It's easy to tell when a person is from the South, from Boston, from Brooklyn and so on just by their pronunciation and intonation of English. The same is true in Latin America. Only occasionally will these variations present a real obstacle to communication.

# ABBREVIATIONS

## Parts of Speech and Other Grammatical Terms

| | |
|---|---|
| adjective | *adj.* |
| adverb | *adv.* |
| article | *art.* |
| conjunction | *conj.* |
| familiar | *fam.* |
| feminine | *f.* |
| formal | *for.* |
| literally | *lit.* |
| masculine | *m.* |
| noun | *n.* |
| plural | *pl.* |
| preposition | *prep.* |
| pronoun | *pron.* |
| singular | *sing.* |
| verb | *v.* |

## Countries and Regions

| | |
|---|---|
| Argentina | *Arg.* |
| Bolivia | *Bol.* |
| Caribbean | *Carib.* |
| Central America | *C.A.* |
| Chile | *Chi.* |
| Colombia | *Col.* |
| Costa Rica | *C.R.* |
| Cuba | *Cuba* |

| | |
|---|---|
| Dominican Republic | *Dom.* |
| Ecuador | *Ec.* |
| El Salvador | *Sal.* |
| Guatemala | *Gua.* |
| Honduras | *Hon.* |
| Latin America | *L.A.* |
| Mexico | *Mex.* |
| Nicaragua | *Nic.* |
| Panama | *Pan.* |
| Paraguay | *Para.* |
| Peru | *Pe.* |
| Puerto Rico | *P.R.* |
| River Plate | *R.P.* |
| South America | *S.A.* |
| Uruguay | *Uru.* |
| Venezuela | *Ven.* |

# TO THE STUDENT

As a longtime teacher of Spanish, I have often heard students say, "I want to learn Spanish, but not the grammar way." However, when I do use a non-grammar approach, the same students are quick to ask, "But why do they say it that way?" This, of course, leads smack dab into an explanation of grammar.

The fact is that most adult students of Spanish feel more secure when they have at least a minimal grasp of the structure, i.e., grammar of the language. We hope that this book will be successful in combining elements of both approaches.

The body of this book begins with two sections that I call "Getting Started—Part 1" and "Getting Started—Part 2." Part One provides a fairly extensive list of basic vocabulary and expressions such as greetings, titles, family relationships, common questions and answers, etc. Part Two contains the numbers and related use of numbers—dates, telling age, and even the conversion of common measurements to the metric system. By learning as much of this material as possible, you will have a considerable base for beginning the lessons that constitute the major part of this book.

Each of the ten lessons in this book begins with a perfectly normal, thoroughly sophisticated dialogue. They reflect the agendas of various types of travelers—tourists, business people, honeymooners, doting grandparents, adventurous young people and so forth. Don't hesitate to plunge right in.

Students of Spanish start out with a couple of important advantages. They already have a wealth of vocabulary under their belts. Who doesn't know such words as *fiesta, siesta, amigo, dinero, sombrero, señor, señora,* not to mention *taco, burrito* and *enchilada?*

Added to that, there are literally thousands of Spanish words that are cognates, words that are the same as or similar to English words. These include words that identify occupations like *doctor, actor, profesor;* adjectives such as *central, cultural, oficial;* animals such as *elefantes, cebras, hipopótamos,* ad infinitum. There is, however, danger in the area of cognates. Some of them are false and can betray you. A classic example is the word *embarazada.* It certainly looks like the English word "embarrassed." In Spanish, however, it means "pregnant."

But don't be afraid to guess at the meanings of words in the opening dialogues. In any case, the dialogues are always followed by their translation to English. That, in turn, is followed by a list of the vocabulary and expressions occurring in the Spanish dialogue.

Spanish words, like words in all languages, rarely have just one meaning. In the lists that follow the dialogues in this book, the translations strictly reflect the meaning of the words as they occur *in those specific dialogues.*

Additional vocabulary, always accompanied by English meaning, is introduced throughout this book in the grammar sections and in the cultural commentaries.

Any of the vocabulary in this book can be looked up in the comprehensive word list provided at the end of the book. The words in this list appear as they would in a standard dictionary—verbs expressed in the infinitive, nouns given with their genders, etc.

The grammar sections of the book provide only the most basic explanations of Spanish structure. They do not include subtleties or extensive listings of exceptions to the rules. You will notice that the number of grammar structures introduced in the lessons varies. In those cases where the structures are more difficult, fewer are included. You will, in these lessons, find a more extensive exercise section. This will provide you with additional practice for the more challenging grammar.

Answers to the exercises will be found at the back of the book.

Also included in each lesson is a section entitled Word Study. This section is aimed at providing tips that will help students to expand their vocabulary.

Each lesson spotlights a specific country or region of Latin America and ends with a brief section I call "A Few Facts About (*name of country*)." The purpose of the section is twofold: 1) To point out the vast diversity, both linguistic and cultural, that exists in the Spanish-speaking world, and 2) To provide a few tidbits that are just plain fun. Language differences included here are in no way exhaustive. It would take a separate book on each country or region to do that.

A few final words about language learning. Don't make it hard on yourself. You don't have to memorize every word and understand every scrap of grammar before moving on. My first foreign language teacher used to say, "Teaching language is like throwing mud at a wall. The first handful, maybe none of it sticks. So you throw another handful and this time a little bit sticks. So you scoop up another handful . . ." Well, you get the idea.

So let me just end this by wishing you ¡*Buena suerte*! in your language learning endeavor. That's "Good luck!" in Spanish.


The Author

# GETTING STARTED—PART 1

So where does one begin? Presumably, of course, at the beginning. But what *is* the beginning when you're tackling a new language?

Mastery of a language ultimately requires that you absorb its entire syntax and acquire an extensive vocabulary to boot. Of the two tasks, conquering the structure is the most difficult. The adding of vocabulary is just an ongoing and never-ending process. But as words are the building blocks of language, that's the logical place to begin. Remember, Tarzan and Jane became acquainted with the simple but now famous words, "Me, Tarzan. You, Jane."

This introductory section provides you with a list of essential words and phrases to get you started down the road. Pronounce, repeat and memorize these words and phrases and they will become a base for the lessons that follow.

## Essential Expressions

The utterly essential words and phrases you'll need to move around Latin America are as follows:

| | |
|---|---|
| Sí | Yes |
| No | No |
| Por favor | Please |
| Gracias | Thank you |
| De nada | You're welcome |

| Perdón | Excuse me |
| Con su permiso | With your permission |

## Greetings

Common greetings include:

| Buenos días. | Good morning. |
| Buenas tardes. | Good afternoon. |
| Buenas noches. | Good evening. |
| ¿Cómo está usted? (for.) | How are you? |
| Hola. (fam.) | Hello, Hi. (fam.) |
| ¿Qué tal? (fam.) | How's it going? (fam.) |

The typical farewells are as follows:

| Adios. | Good-bye. |
| Hasta luego. | See you later. |
| Hasta mañana. | See you tomorrow. |
| Buenas noches. | Good night. |
| Chau. | Ciao. (A familiar Italian greeting to say hello/good-bye, and commonly used in Latin America.) |

## The Formal and Familiar "You"

With certain exceptions, Latin Americans tend to be rather formal in how they address one another. One of the ways they communicate the formality or informality of relationships is by their use of either the informal word for "you," *tú,* or the formal word, *usted,* often abbreviated as *Ud.* A number of languages have this characteristic as did English at one time. The words "thee" and "thou" were our informal words for "you." Today, however, they have fallen out of general usage and are only found in poetry and prayers or used by certain religious groups.

The use of *tú* and *usted* in the Spanish-speaking world is a delicate matter. Judging relationships in social situations requires a thorough knowledge of the mores of the specific country. Therefore, it's strongly advised that beginners in Spanish limit themselves to using *usted.* It is ever so much better to be too formal than to be too familiar.

Although the familiar *tú* forms are not taught in this book, they do occur in the dialogues. For example, a honeymoon couple would obviously not address one another as *usted.*

All the informal forms that appear in the dialogues are labeled (*fam.*) and will provide students with the opportunity to familiarize themselves with the forms while making no attempt to master them.

## Titles

As a part of that formality of Latin America, you'll find that titles are used more liberally than they are in the northern part of the Western Hemisphere. Among the common ones are:

| | |
|---|---|
| Señor | Mr., sir |
| Señora | Mrs., madam |

| | |
|---|---|
| Señorita | Miss |
| Profesor | Professor (*m.*) |
| Profesora | Professor (*f.*) |
| Doctor | Doctor (*m.*) |
| Doctora | Doctor (*f.*) |

You'll also find that Latin Americans address professionals such as lawyers, engineers and architects by titles. They are as follows:

| | |
|---|---|
| licenciado | lawyer |
| ingeniero | engineer |
| arquitecto | architect |

## Family Relationships

The extended family is the backbone of the Hispanic culture. For this reason, one of the first inquiries that a person will make in a social situation is "How's the family?" or *¿Cómo está la familia?*

The names of the various family members are as follows:

| | |
|---|---|
| madre, mamá | mother, mom |
| padre, papá | father, dad |
| hijo | son |
| hija | daughter |
| padres | parents |
| esposa | wife |
| esposo | husband |
| hermana | sister |
| hermano | brother |

| abuela | grandmother |
| abuelo | grandfather |
| tía | aunt |
| tío | uncle |
| prima | cousin (f.) |
| primo | cousin (m.) |
| sobrina | niece |
| sobrino | nephew |
| nieta | granddaughter |
| nieto | grandson |
| parientes | relatives |
| familia | family |

## Common Questions, Answers and Other Expressions

| | |
| --- | --- |
| ¿Cómo se llama usted? | What's your name? |
| Me llamo _____. | My name is _____. |
| *or* | (I call myself...) |
| Mi nombre es _____. | My name is _____. |
| ¿Cómo está usted? | How are you? |
| Bien, gracias. | Fine, thanks. |
| ¿Qué tal? | How's it going? |
| Muy bien. | Very well. |
| Quiero presentarle a... | I'd like to introduce you to... |
| Mucho gusto. | Pleased to meet you. |
| El gusto es mío. | The pleasure is mine. |
| ¿Cómo se dice esto? | How do you say—? |
| | (*point to object*) |
| ¿Habla usted inglés? | Do you speak English? |
| Yo hablo español un poco. | I speak a little Spanish. |

| Hable más despacio, | Speak more slowly, |
|---|---|
| por favor. | please. |

## Practice

Respond to the following in Spanish:

1. Buenas tardes.

2. ¿Qué tal?

3. ¿Cómo está usted?

4. ¿Cómo se llama usted?

5. Hasta luego.

6. ¡Hola!

7. ¿Cómo está la familia?

What would be the appropriate thing to say in Spanish in the following situations?

1. You're greeting a coworker when you arrive at work.

2. You want to say "Hi" to a neighbor.

3. You're asking a friend's father "How are you?"

4. You want to say "good-bye," but in a very informal manner.

5. It's evening and you're saying a formal "good-bye."

# GETTING STARTED—PART 2

## The Numbers

As essential as the vocabulary and expressions in Part I are the numbers and their applications.

Understanding taxi fares, negotiating a business deal, bartering in the market, making a phone call or setting up an appointment all require a knowledge of the numbers.

The following are the cardinal numbers in Spanish from zero through fifteen:

| | | | | | |
|---|---|---|---|---|---|
| 0 | cero | | | | |
| 1 | uno | 6 | seis | 11 | once |
| 2 | dos | 7 | siete | 12 | doce |
| 3 | tres | 8 | ocho | 13 | trece |
| 4 | cuatro | 9 | nueve | 14 | catorce |
| 5 | cinco | 10 | diez | 15 | quince |

## *Practice*

Give the answers to the following math problems:

1. $1 \times 1 =$
2. $2 + 4 =$
3. $7 + 7 =$
4. $3 \times 5 =$
5. $7 - 3 =$
6. $15 - 5 =$

The simplest, though not the only way, of reading telephone numbers is just to read them one digit at a time. Thus, the number 828-1245 would be said *ocho-dos-ocho-uno-dos-cuatro-cinco.*

**Practice**

Read the following telephone numbers in Spanish:

1. 894-6723

2. 685-2931

3. 893-2150

4. 905-6130

5. 284-3390

6. 442-0589

7. Your own telephone number

The area code is referred to as *la área* and can be read in the same way, by its digits. Thus, (212) 865-2092 would be read: *la área dos-uno-dos ocho-seis-cinco dos-cero-nueve-dos.*

## Cardinal Numbers 16 through 30

| | |
|---|---|
| 16 | diez y seis |
| 17 | diez y siete |
| 18 | diez y ocho |
| 19 | diez y nueve |

| 20 | veinte |
| 21 | veinte y uno |
| 22 | veinte y dos |
| 23 | veinte y tres |
| 24 | veinte y cuatro |
| 25 | veinte y cinco |
| 26 | veinte y seis |
| 27 | veinte y siete |
| 28 | veinte y ocho |
| 29 | veinte y nueve |
| 30 | treinta |

These numbers are sometimes written as one word. For example, the number 16 can be written either *diez y seis* or *dieciséis*. The one-word spelling is usually only used up through 29.

The numbers from sixteen through the nineties can be formed by using the *ten*-words and adding the appropriate digit. Thus 39 is "thirty and nine" or *treinta y nueve*.

The *ten*-words from 20 through 90 are as follows:

| 20 | veinte |
| 30 | treinta |
| 40 | cuarenta |
| 50 | cincuenta |
| 60 | sesenta |
| 70 | setenta |
| 80 | ochenta |
| 90 | noventa |

## Practice

Read the following numbers in Spanish:

| | | | |
|---|---|---|---|
| 1. | 46 | 4. | 66 |
| 2. | 73 | 5. | 91 |
| 3. | 32 | 6. | 54 |

# The Cardinal Numbers through 1000

One hundred, when it stands alone, is *cien*, but when it is followed by other numbers it is *ciento*. So 101 is *ciento uno*. Beginning with 116, the pattern is "one hundred ten and six," or *ciento diez y seis*. The same pattern is followed throughout the hundreds, the little word *y* always going between the tens and the digits, not between the hundreds and the tens.

The hundreds are as follows:

| | |
|---|---|
| 100 | cien |
| 200 | doscientos |
| 300 | trescientos |
| 400 | cuatrocientos |
| 500 | quinientos |
| 600 | seiscientos |
| 700 | setecientos |
| 800 | ochocientos |
| 900 | novecientos |

The word for 1000 in Spanish is *mil*. So to read dates just break it down as follows: 1932 would be read as "one thousand nine-hundred thirty and two" or *mil novecientos treinta y dos*.

The word for a "million" in Spanish is *millón*. It's considered a noun in Spanish and is always followed by the word "of," or *de*, before a noun, as in "a million (of) dollars," or *un millón de dólares*. The same holds true for "a billion," so "a billion (of) dollars" would be *un billón de dólares*.

An interesting number fact is that a billion in the United States and Canada is a thousand million whereas in Latin America it's a million million. A rather important difference.

Now you can read even the big numbers just by breaking them down. Here's an example. Break down the number 5,426,987 as follows:

"Five million-four hundred twenty and six thousand-nine hundred eighty and seven," which in Spanish will be read *cinco millones-cuatrocientos veinte y seis mil-novecientos ochenta y siete*.

## Practice

Read the following numbers in Spanish:

1. 362          6. 1,387

2. 596          7. 5,376

3. 187          8. 3,942,345

4. 963          9. 27,531,643

5. 416

The way to read the year is the same as any other number. If the year is 1996 you say: "one thousand-nine hundred-ninety and six" or, in Spanish, *mil novecientos noventa y seis*. We have now passed into a new millennium and, at the time of this writing, are beginning the year 2001, or *dos mil uno*.

## *Practice*

Read the following years in Spanish:

1.  1938

2.  2000

3.  1810

4.  1940

5.  1776

6.  The year Columbus discovered America

7.  The year of your birth

# The Ordinal Numbers

To say "first," "second," "third" and so forth use the ordinal numbers, as follows:

|           |        |
| --------- | ------ |
| primer(o) | first  |
| segundo   | second |
| tercer(o) | third  |
| cuarto    | fourth |
| quinto    | fifth  |
| sexto     | sixth  |

| | |
|---|---|
| séptimo | seventh |
| octavo | eighth |
| noveno | ninth |
| décimo | tenth |

The ordinal numbers end in *o* when they precede a noun ending in *o*. They end in *a* when they precede a noun ending in *a*. The ordinal numbers *primero* and *tercero* drop the *o* when they precede a noun ending in *o*. (More on agreement of adjectives in Lesson 2.)

## *Practice*

Fill in the ordinal number in Spanish:

1. la (sixth) _____ familia

2. el (third) _____ esposo

3. el (fifth) _____ ingeniero

4. la (ninth) _____ profesora

5. el (second) _____ hijo

## The Calendar

To read a complete date, you need to know not only the numbers but also the days of the week and the months of the year. The days of the week are:

| | |
|---|---|
| domingo | Sunday |
| lunes | Monday |

| martes | Tuesday |
| miércoles | Wednesday |
| jueves | Thursday |
| viernes | Friday |
| sábado | Saturday |

The months of the year are:

| enero | January |
| febrero | February |
| marzo | March |
| abril | April |
| mayo | May |
| junio | June |
| julio | July |
| agosto | August |
| septiembre | September |
| octubre | October |
| noviembre | November |
| diciembre | December |

Thus, you read the date "Tuesday, December 25, 1999," as "Tuesday, 25 of December of 1999," or *martes, el veinte y cinco de diciembre de mil novecientos noventa y nueve.*

### Practice

Read the following dates in Spanish:

1.   Monday, January 26, 1952

2.   Thursday, July 7, 1856

3.  Saturday, August 16, 2001

4.  Sunday, December 7, 1941

5.  Today's date

## Telling Time

Spanish speakers say, "What hour is it?" rather than "What time is it?" With the exception of 1:00 and its subdivisions, the plural is always used. For 1:00 the verb used is *es*; from 2:00 through 12:00 the verb *son* is used. The *la* and *las* forms are feminine as they agree with the understood words *hora* and *horas*.

>   *¿Qué hora es?*
>   What time is it?

>   *¿Qué horas son? (Mex.)*
>   *Es la una.*
>   It's one o'clock.

>   *Son las dos.*
>   It's two o'clock.

To add minutes after the hour, just add *y* and the number of minutes. At the quarter hour, you can add the word "quarter," or *cuarto*. At the half hour you can say "half" or *media*.

>   *Son las dos y veinte.*
>   It's two twenty.

>   *Son las dos y cuarto.*
>   It's two fifteen.

*Son las dos y media.*
It's two thirty.

To tell the minutes it is before the next hour, you say that hour
and subtract the number of minutes. Thus "20 minutes to four"
(or 3:40) is "four minus twenty":

*Son las cuatro menos veinte.*
It's 3:40.

*Son las diez menos cuarto.*
It's a quarter to 9:00.

## Time Related Vocabulary and Expressions

| | |
|---|---|
| segundos | seconds |
| minutos | minutes |
| horas | hours |
| mañana | morning |
| tarde | afternoon |
| noche | evening, night |
| de la mañana | A.M. |
| de la tarde | P.M. |
| de la noche | (same) |
| ¿A qué hora? | (At) what time? |
| a tiempo | on time |
| ayer | yesterday |
| hoy | today |
| mañana | tomorrow |
| día | day |
| mes | month |
| año | year |

## *Practice*

Read the following times in Spanish:

1.   8:10 P.M.

2.   6:15 A.M.

3.   1:00 P.M.

4.   2:30

5.   4:25

6.   4:45

7.   11:40

## Telling Your Age

To tell your age, you say "I have *(so many)* years." Thus, someone asking your age will say, "How many years do you have?":

> *¿Cuántos años tiene usted?*     How old are you?

You will answer, "I have _____ years" or *Tengo* _____ *años.*

# The Metric System

As all of Latin America is on the metric system of weights and measurements, you'll need to know a few equivalents. Here are some of the basic ones:

| | | |
|---|---|---|
| 1 kilo | = | 2.2 pounds |
| 1 liter (litro) | = | 1.1 quarts |
| 3.785 liters (litros) | = | 1 gallon |
| 0 Centigrade (centígrado) | = | 32 Fahrenheit (freezing) |
| 37 Centigrade | = | 98.6 Fahrenheit (body temperature) |
| 1 centimeter (centímetro) | = | .39 inches |
| 2.54 centimeter | = | 1 inch |
| 1 kilometer (kilómetro) | = | 0.62 miles |

LESSON

1

# En el Aeropuerto

## Diálogo

*El señor Ortega, un hombre de negocios que vive en San Antonio, llega al aeropuerto Benito Juárez de México, D. F. (Distrito Federal), para reunirse con su socio mexicano:*

**Sr. Ortega:** Señorita ¿A dónde voy para reclamar mi equipaje?

**Empleada de la aereolínea Mexicana:** Siga usted a esa gente a migración. Allí puede reclamar su equipaje y también puede pasar por migración y la aduana. Si tiene sus papeles listos va más rápido.

**Sr. Ortega:** Muchas gracias.

*En migración, el señor Ortega presenta sus papeles de viajero y el oficial les pone sello.*

*De allí, va a la aduana. En los aeropuertos internacionales en México hay un sistema en que el viajero empuja un botón y si sale la luz verde, no tiene que pasar por inspección aduanal. Si sale la luz roja, tiene que pasar por la inspección. Le toca al señor Ortega la luz roja:*

**Oficial de Aduana:** Buenas tardes. ¿Tiene usted algo que declarar?

**Sr. Ortega:** No, no tengo nada que declarar. Todo es para mi uso personal. Puedo abrir mi maleta, si usted quiere.

# In the Airport

## *Dialogue*

*Mr. Ortega, a businessman who lives in San Antonio, arrives in the Benito Juárez airport in Mexico City to meet with his Mexican partner:*

**Mr. Ortega:** Miss, where do I go to claim my luggage?

**Mexicana airlines employee:** Follow those people to immigration. There you can claim your luggage and also go through immigration and customs. If you have your papers ready, it will go faster.

**Mr. Ortega:** Thanks a lot.

*In immigration, Mr. Ortega presents his travel papers and the official puts a stamp on them.*

*From there, he goes to customs. In the international airports in Mexico, there is a system in which the traveler pushes a button and if a green light comes on he doesn't have to go through inspection. If the red light comes on, he does have to go through inspection. Mr. Ortega gets the red light:*

**Customs official:** Good afternoon. Do you have anything to declare?

**Mr. Ortega:** No, I don't have anything to declare. Everything is for my personal use. I can open my suitcase if you want.

**Oficial de Aduana:** No es necesario, señor. Pase usted.

*Afuera, el socio mexicano del señor Ortega, el señor Sandoval, lo espera. Un socio suyo, el señor Dávila, le acompaña:*

**Sr. Sandoval:** Bienvenido a México. ¿Qué tal fue el viaje?

**Sr. Ortega:** Muy bien. Qué gusto verlo otra vez.

**Sr. Sandoval:** Quiero presentarle a un socio mío, el licenciado Dávila.

**Sr. Ortega:** Mucho gusto.

**Sr. Dávila:** El gusto es mío.

**Sr. Sandoval:** Voy a buscar el carro para ir a su hotel. Allí podemos comer y hablar un poco.

**Sr. Ortega:** Sí, siempre es bueno llegar. Qué bonito es el aeropuerto después de su remodelación.

**Sr. Sandoval:** Es verdad. Y es más cómodo también.

**Sr. Ortega:** Sí, pero hay un problema. Sin todas esas escaleras de antes, ya no hago nada de ejercicio.

**Customs official:** No, it's not necessary, sir. Go on through.

*Outside, Mr. Ortega's Mexican partner, Mr. Sandoval, is waiting for him. An associate of his, Mr. Dávila, is with him:*

**Mr. Sandoval:** Welcome to Mexico. How was the trip?

**Mr. Ortega:** Just fine. What a pleasure to see you again!

**Mr. Sandoval:** I want to present to you an associate of mine, *Licenciado* Dávila.

**Mr. Ortega:** (It's) a pleasure to meet you.

**Mr. Dávila:** The pleasure is mine.

**Mr. Sandoval:** I'm going for the car to go to your hotel. There we can eat and talk a little.

**Mr. Ortega:** Yes, it's always good to arrive. How pretty the airport is after its remodeling.

**Mr. Sandoval:** That's true. And it's more comfortable, too.

**Mr. Ortega:** But there's a problem. Without all those stairs (that were) here before, I don't get (do) any exercise anymore.

## Vocabulary

| | |
|---|---|
| ¿A dónde? | (To) where . . .? |
| a | to |
| abrir | to open |
| aduana | customs |
| aerolínea | airline |
| aeropuerto | airport |
| afuera | outside |
| al | to the |
| algo | something |
| allí | there |
| bienvenido | welcome |
| bonito | pretty |
| botón | button |
| bueno | good |
| buscar | look for |
| comer | to eat |
| cómodo | comfortable |
| con | with |
| de antes | here before |
| de | of, from |
| declarar | to declare |
| del | of the |
| después de | after |
| ejercicio | exercise |
| el | the (m.) |
| empleada | employee (f.) |
| empuja | pushes |
| en | in |
| equipaje | luggage |
| es | is |

| esa | that |
|-----|------|
| esas | those |
| escaleras | stairs |
| espera | waits for |
| está | is |
| este | this |
| gente | people |
| gracias | thanks |
| hablar | to talk |
| hago | I get (do) |
| hay | there is |
| hombre | man |
| hotel | hotel |
| imigración | immigration |
| inspección | inspection |
| ir | to go |
| la | the (f.) |
| le toca | he gets to (it's his turn) |
| les | them |
| licenciado | (title for a lawyer or person with a university degree) |
| listos | ready |
| llega | arrives |
| llegar | to arrive, to get there |
| lo | him, it |
| luz | light |
| maleta | suitcase |
| más | more |
| mexicano | Mexican |
| mi | my |
| mío | of mine |

| | |
|---|---|
| muchas | many |
| nada | nothing |
| necesario | necessary |
| negocios | business |
| no | no |
| oficial | official |
| otra vez | once again |
| papeles | papers |
| para | (in order) to |
| pasar | to go through |
| pase | pass (on through) |
| personal | personal |
| poner | to put |
| presentar | to present |
| presentarle | to introduce someone |
| puede | you can |
| que | which, what, that (as connector) |
| ¿qué? | how? what? |
| quiere | you want |
| quiero | I want |
| rápido | fast |
| reclamar | to claim |
| remodelación | remodeling |
| roja | red |
| sale | goes out |
| señor | Mister, sir |
| señorita | Miss |
| si | if |
| sí | yes, indeed |
| siempre | always |
| siga | follow |
| sin | without |

| | |
|---|---|
| sistema | system |
| socio | partner, associate |
| solamente | only |
| su | its, your |
| sus | her/his, your (*pl.*) |
| suyo | of his |
| también | too, also |
| taxi | taxi |
| tiene que | it/she/he has to |
| tiene | you have |
| todas | all |
| todo | everything |
| un | a (*m.*, *art.*) |
| uso | use |
| usted (abbr. Ud.) | you (*for.*) |
| va a ser | it's going to be |
| va | it/she/he goes |
| vamos | let's go |
| verde | green |
| verle | to see you |
| viajero | traveler |
| vivir | to live |
| voy | I go |
| y | and |
| ya | already |

## *Expressions*

| | |
|---|---|
| Buenas tardes. | Good afternoon. |
| El gusto es mío. | The pleasure is mine. |

| | |
|---|---|
| Mucho gusto. | My pleasure. |
| Muy bien. | Very well. |
| Qué gusto. | What a pleasure. |
| ¿Qué tal fue? | How was it? |

# Grammar

## Subject Pronouns

In Spanish, the pronouns that are used as the subjects of sentences are the following:

| yo | I | nosotros | we (*m.*) |
| | | nosotras | we (*f.*) |
| él | he | ellos | they (*m.*) |
| ella | she | ellas | they (*f.*) |
| usted | you (*for.*) | ustedes | you (*pl.*) |

Unlike English, the subject pronouns are often not used in Spanish. As Spanish is a highly inflected language, the endings of the verbs often make it clear who the speaker is. In those cases where there could be confusion, however, it is always appropriate to use them.

The familiar forms for "you," both singular and plural, *tú* and *vosotros*, are roughly equivalent to the English words "thee" and "thou" which have fallen out of usage except in certain religious communities, prayers and poetry. Their equivalents in Spanish, however, are used extensively, particularly the *tú* form. It is recommended, however, that persons with limited knowledge of Spanish always use the formal "you" in Spanish in order to avoid unintentionally giving offense. For that reason, only the formal forms, *usted* and *ustedes*, are included in the grammar sections of this book.

## Regular -ar Verbs

Regular verbs in Spanish are those that follow consistent patterns throughout all their tenses. They fall into three categories. The infinitives all end in either -ar, -er or -ir. The infinitives are those forms of the verbs that are equivalent to "to" plus the verb in English as in "to claim" which in Spanish is *reclamar*. The present tense of *reclamar* is as follows:

| | |
|---|---|
| yo reclamo | I claim |
| él/ella/usted reclama | he/she/you (for.) claim(s) |
| nosotros/-as reclamamos | we claim |
| ellos/ellas/ustedes reclaman | they (m. and f.)/you (pl.) claim |

Common regular -ar verbs that follow the same pattern as the above include:

| | |
|---|---|
| llegar | to arrive |
| hablar | to talk |
| llamar | to call |
| comprar | to buy |
| cambiar | to change, exchange |
| preguntar | to ask (a question) |
| caminar | to walk |
| necesitar | to need |
| trabajar | to work |
| estudiar | to study |
| bailar | to dance |
| cantar | to sing |
| invitar | to invite |
| visitar | to visit |

| viajar | to travel |
| entrar | to enter |
| esperar | to wait (for) |

As -ar verbs constitute the majority of regular verbs in Spanish, a working knowledge of this conjugation in its most essential tenses will be very useful.

## Gender of Nouns

In Spanish, every noun—including inanimate objects—is either masculine or feminine. Usually (there are a few exceptions) nouns ending in o are masculine and nouns ending in a are feminine. The gender of nouns that end in some other letter simply must be learned as vocabulary acquisition progresses. Physical gender generally does apply to animate beings regardless of word ending when the gender is obvious:

| el hombre | the man |
| la mujer | the woman |
| el muchacho | the boy |
| la muchacha | the girl |

Among the exceptions mentioned above are a series of words that end in a but are masculine. Some of the more common ones are the following:

| el problema | the problem |
| el sistema | the system |
| el clima | the climate |

| | |
|---|---|
| el programa | the program |
| el día | the day |

There are a few words that end in *o* but are feminine. One of the most common is *la mano* (the hand).

In learning the gender of nouns it's helpful to know that there are a series of endings that always indicate that a noun is feminine. They are *-ción, -sión, -dad, -tad* and *-umbre.* Examples:

| | |
|---|---|
| la televisión | television |
| la ciudad | city |
| la libertad | liberty |
| la legumbre | vegetable |

## Definite and Indefinite Articles

The definite article "the" in Spanish has four forms, masculine singular *el*, masculine plural *los*, feminine singular *la* and feminine plural *las*:

| | |
|---|---|
| el aeropuerto | the airport |
| la maleta | the suitcase |
| los aeropuertos | the airports |
| las maletas | the suitcases |

The indefinite articles "a" and "an" are *un* (*m.*) and *una* (*f.*) in the singular.

| | |
|---|---|
| un aeropuerto | an airport |
| una maleta | a suitcase |

When *un* is pluralized to *unos* and *una* to *unas,* the meaning is "some."

| | |
|---|---|
| unos aeropuertos | some airports |
| unas maletas | some suitcases |

## Plural of Nouns

The pluralization of nouns in Spanish is a simple matter. You simply add *-s* to nouns ending in a vowel and *-es* to nouns ending in a consonant.

| | |
|---|---|
| aeropuerto | aeropuertos |
| hotel | hoteles |

One small deviation to this rule is when a noun ends in *z*, the *z* changes to a *c* and is then followed by *–es*.

| | | | |
|---|---|---|---|
| *luz* | light | *luces* | lights |

When an *-es* is added to a noun, a written accent may no longer be necessary. Review the rules on stress and you will see how the addition of a syllable may eliminate the need for a written accent.

| | |
|---|---|
| inspección | inspecciones |

## Making Sentences Negative

To make a Spanish sentence negative, just put *no* before the verb:

> *Necesito reclamar mi equipaje.*
> I need to claim my luggage.

> <u>No</u> *necesito reclamar mi equipaje.*
> I don't need to claim my luggage.

## Questions

The most usual way to form a question in Spanish is to invert the subject and the verb of the sentence:

> *El señor Ortega es de San Antonio.*
> Mr. Ortega is from San Antonio.

> *¿Es el señor Ortega de San Antonio?*
> Is Mr. Ortega from San Antonio?

It is also possible to make a statement and then inflect it as a question:

> *José come en el hotel.*
> José eats in the hotel.

> *¿José come en el hotel?*
> José eats in the hotel?

Still another way to ask a question is to make a statement and then follow it with the words *¿verdad?* or simply *¿no?* These tag endings are equivalent to the English "right?" For example:

*El aeropuerto es muy cómodo ¿verdad?*
The airport is very comfortable, right?

*El aeropuerto es muy cómodo ¿no?*
The airport is very comfortable, right?

## Exercises

I.  Express the following in Spanish:

1. I                    5. he
2. they (*f.*)          6. you (*pl.*)
3. she                  7. you (*for., sing.*)
4. we (*m.*)            8. they (*f.*)

II. Fill in the blank with the correct present tense form of the verb in parentheses:

1. El señor Ortega (reclamar) _____ su equipaje en la aduana.

2. Nosotros (presentar) _____ los papeles en migración.

3. Los hombres de negocio (llegar) _____ al aeropuerto frecuentemente.

4. Ellos (buscar) _____ el carro para ir al hotel.

5. El señor Sandoval (esperar) _____ en la sala de espera.

III. Read the following nouns with their corresponding *definite* articles:

1. hotel              6. carro
2. maleta             7. viaje
3. uso                8. inspección
4. socio              9. botón
5. luz               10. oficial

IV. Now read the above list with their corresponding *indefinite* articles.

V. Read the following nouns in the plural:

1. el papel
2. la maleta
3. la sala
4. el carro
5. el socio

6. la remodelación
7. el hotel
8. la luz
9. el hombre
10. el botón

VI. Change the following sentences to the negative:

1. Podemos comer en el hotel.

2. El señor Ortega es hombre de negocios.

3. El señor Sandoval es socio del señor Dávila.

4. El señor Ortega espera al señor Sandoval.

5. El oficial de migración pone sello en los papeles de viajero.

VII. Change the following statements to questions:

1. El señor Ortega presenta sus papeles en migración.

2. Ellos reclaman el equipaje en la aduana.

3. Usted tiene sus papeles listos.

4. El señor Ortega llega al aeropuerto de México.

5. Usted tiene algo que declarar.

## Word Study

The first step that beginning students should take is to inventory all the Spanish vocabulary they already have and then assess and polish it. Most English speakers have no problem pronouncing such Spanish words as *siesta, fiesta, taco* and *peso.* They have more difficulty with the purity of Spanish vowels in such words as *burro,* whose first syllable should be pronounced "boo," and *sombrero,* whose first syllable should be pronounced "sohm."

The pronunciation of Hispanic names is often difficult for English speakers who will say, for example, *MAR-ti-nez* instead of *Mar-TI-nez* or *Cha-VEZ* instead of *CHA-vez.* Nor are the problems limited to issues of accent and stress. A name like *Velásquez* is often incorrectly pronounced as "Vay-LAHS-kways" rather than "Vay-LAHS-kays."

The mispronunciation of names can lead to practical problems. One Spanish speaker tells how she was waiting to see her doctor and wondering why her turn was so long in coming. She came to find out that the receptionist had called her name but that she hadn't recognized it. Her name was Villareal, a relatively common Hispanic surname, and the receptionist had pronounced it "Villa-" (as in "lavish country estate") and "real" (as in "the diamonds are real"). And this problem is more common that one might think. It happens every day in hospitals, doctors' offices and other agencies.

English speakers, of course, face the same problem when they travel to Spanish-speaking countries. When paged in airports and hotels they often fail to recognize their names as pronounced.

By applying the rules of pronunciation outlined in the introductory materials in the book, students can do much to
improve their already existent vocabulary base. It's not easy to
break long-standing habits, but it's well worth the effort.

## A Few Facts About Mexico

Within the country of Mexico, Mexicans refer to Mexico City as simply *México*.

A city bus in Mexico is called a *camión* which in most Spanish-speaking countries means a "truck."

If you want to ask for peanuts you need to request *cacahuates*, an Indian word. The rest of the Spanish-speaking world says *maní*.

Try not to miss sampling the best known regional food dishes of Mexico. They're much more varied than what is known as "Mexican" food outside of Mexico. For instance, in the State of Jalisco try the *pozole*, a spicy pork and hominy stew. The State of Puebla is famous for its chicken *mole*, that's chicken in a sauce of bitter chocolate, chile and a blend of spices. On the Gulf of Mexico in the State of Veracruz people are fond of *huachinango a la veracruzana*, red snapper in a tomato, onion, olive and caper sauce. And of course, you may want to wash all this down with good Mexican *tequila*.

LESSON
2

# En el Hotel

## Diálogo

*Los jóvenes mexicanos, Jorge y Luisa, recién casados, llegan a Cuba para su luna de miel. Están registrándose en el hotel de lujo Meliá Habana:*

**Jorge:** Buenos días. Tenemos reservación para habitación doble en nombre de Jorge Vega.

**Recepcionista:** Sí, señor Vega. Ustedes están en la habitación 1214 (doce catorce). El botones tiene la llave y va a subir su equipaje. Los elevadores están a la derecha.

**Jorge:** ¿Y dónde está el restaurante?

**Recepcionista:** Está a la izquierda; da al lobby.

**Jorge:** ¿Hay servicio a la habitación?

**Recepcionista:** Claro que sí, señor.

**Luisa:** ¿Hay salón de belleza aquí?

**Recepcionista:** Sí, señora. Hay una buena peluquería aquí. Así se llaman en Cuba.

**Jorge:** Ay, mi vida, no vas (*fam.*) a necesitar salón de belleza. Para mí, siempre estás (*fam.*) bonita.

# In the Hotel

## *Dialogue*

*The young Mexicans, Jorge and Luisa, newlyweds, arrive in Cuba on their honeymoon. They are checking into the luxurious Meliá Habana hotel:*

**Jorge:** Good morning. I have a reservation for two here. My name is Jorge Vega.

**Desk clerk:** Yes, Mr. Vega. You're in room number 1214. The bellboy has the keys and will bring up your luggage. The elevators are to the right.

**Jorge:** Where is the restaurant?

**Desk clerk:** It's to your left, right off the lobby.

**Jorge:** Is there room service?

**Desk clerk:** Of course.

**Louisa:** And is there a beauty salon here?

**Desk clerk:** Yes, madam. There's a good beauty salon (*peluquería*) here, that's what we call them in Cuba.

**Jorge:** Oh, honey, you're not going to need a beauty salon. To me, you're always pretty.

**Recepcionista:** Otros servicios que ofrecemos incluyen cambio de dinero, tienda de regalos, barbería y lavandería. Si ustedes necesitan algo más, llamen a la recepción.

**Jorge:** Muchas gracias. Usted es muy amable.

*En la habitación:*

**Jorge:** ¡Esta habitación no tiene cama matrimonial!

**Botones:** El hotel puede cambiarla. No se preocupe.

*Solos, al fin:*

**Luisa:** Ay, Jorge. Quiero mucho salir a conocer este país tan lindo y a su pueblo.

**Jorge:** Pero mi vida, para hacer eso, vamos a tener que salir de la habitación.

**Desk clerk:** Other services we offer include a money exchange, a gift shop, a barbershop and laundry. If you need anything else, call the reception desk.

**Jorge:** Thanks a lot. You're very kind.

*In the room:*

**Jorge:** This room doesn't have a double bed!

**Bellboy:** The hotel can change it. Don't worry.

*Alone at last:*

**Luisa:** Oh, Jorge. I want so much to go out and get to know this beautiful country and its people.

**Jorge:** But honey, (in order) to do that, we're going to have to leave the room.

## Vocabulary

| | |
|---|---|
| a la izquierda | to the left |
| a | in |
| al fin | finally |
| algo | anything |
| amable | kind |
| aquí | here |
| así | thus |
| ay | oh |
| barbería | barbershop |
| bonita | pretty |
| botones | bellboy |
| buena | good |
| cama matrimonial | double bed |
| cambiarla | change it |
| cambio de dinero | money exchange |
| conocer | to get acquainted with |
| da al lobby | it's off the lobby |
| de lujo | luxurious |
| ¿dónde? | where? |
| elevadores | elevators |
| en | on |
| equipaje | luggage |
| eres | you are (*fam.*) |
| eso | that |
| espero | I hope |
| está | is |
| esta | this |
| están | they are |
| estás | you are (*fam.*) |
| este | this |

| habitación | room |
|---|---|
| hacer | to do |
| ¿Hay—? | Is there—? |
| hotel | hotel |
| incluyen | they include |
| jóvenes | young people |
| lavandería | laundry |
| llamen | call |
| llave | key |
| llegan | they arrive |
| luna de miel | honeymoon |
| más | more |
| mexicanos | Mexican |
| mi vida | honey (literally "my life") |
| muy | very |
| no tiene | doesn't have |
| no vas a necesitar | you're not going to need (fam.) |
| otros | other |
| país | country |
| para | for, in order to |
| para hacer eso | in order to do that |
| para mí | to (for) me |
| peluquería | beauty shop (Cuba) |
| pero | but |
| pueblo | people |
| puede | can |
| que | that |
| quiero | I want |
| recepción | reception desk |
| recién casados | newlyweds |
| registrándose | registering |

| | |
|---|---|
| reservación | reservation |
| restaurante | restaurant |
| salir | to go out |
| salón de belleza | beauty shop |
| se llaman | they're called |
| servicio a la habitación | room service |
| servicios | services |
| si | if |
| siempre | always |
| solos | alone |
| su | their, your, its |
| tan lindo | so pretty |
| tanto | so much |
| tenemos | we have |
| tener que salir (de) | to have to leave |
| tienda de regalos | gift shop |
| tiene | has |
| Usted es | you are |
| Ustedes necesitan | you need (pl.) |
| va a subir | he's going to take up |
| vamos a | we are going to |

## Expressions

| | |
|---|---|
| Claro que sí. | Certainly. |
| No se preocupe. | Don't worry. |

# Grammar

## Present Tense of ser

There are a number of verbs in Spanish that are irregular, that is, their forms do not follow the regular pattern throughout all their tenses. Among the most basic ones are the two verbs "to be," *ser* and *estar*. As they follow no set pattern, they must simply be memorized.

This lesson introduces the verb *ser*, "to be." This verb is used to express identity (I am Manuel), place of origin (I am from Peru), occupation (I am an accountant) and nationality (I am Peruvian). When followed by an adjective, it indicates a permanent characteristic. (Snow is cold. Manuel is intelligent.)

*Ser* is also the verb used in telling time. (It's one o'clock. It's a quarter to nine.)

Its present tense forms are:

| | |
|---|---|
| yo soy | I am |
| el/ella/usted es | he/she is, you (*for.*) are |
| nosotros/-as somos | we are |
| ellos/ellas/ustedes son | they/you (*pl.*) are |

## Possession with de

Possession of a noun by another noun in Spanish is indicated by using the preposition *de* followed by the possessor. For example, "Luisa's suitcase" would be "the suitcase of Luisa" or *la maleta de Luisa*. When the article *el* follows the preposition *de* it contracts to *del*. So "a service of the hotel" is *un servicio del hotel*.

The apostrophe is not used in Spanish to indicate possession.

## Adjectives

In Spanish, adjectives—those words that describe or limit nouns—must agree with the nouns they modify in both gender and number. Thus, adjectives that end in *o* become feminine by changing the ending to *a*. Example: *el viajero mexicano* will become *la viajera mexicana* if, in fact, the traveler is a woman. If the noun is plural as in *viajeros* the article becomes *los* and the adjective *mexicano* becomes *mexicanos.* The phrase then is *los viajeros mexicanos*. The feminine plural would be *las viajeras mexicanas*.

The same form of the adjective is used for both masculine and feminine if it ends in *e* or a consonant: *el señor amable, la señora amable.*

If the article modifies plural nouns of both genders, the masculine prevails. Example: "Mr. and Mrs. García" are *los señores García*.

Several common adjectives have special characteristics. They are *bueno* (good), and *malo* (bad). *Buen(o)* and *mal(o)* can go either before or after the noun they modify. However, if placed before a masculine singular noun, the final *o* is dropped:

|                  |     |                 |
|------------------|-----|-----------------|
| un hombre bueno  | or  | un buen hombre  |
| un hombre malo   | or  | un mal hombre   |

The adjective *grande* means both "great" and "large." If placed before the noun, it drops the final *-de* and means "great." If it follows the noun, it remains *grande* and means "big" or "large." Examples:

| | |
|---|---|
| el gran hombre | the great man |
| el hombre grande | the big man |

You'll note that a major difference between English and Spanish is that, in Spanish, descriptive adjectives usually follow the noun. Limiting adjectives—definite and indefinite articles, numbers, etc.—normally go before. Thus, "a pretty young lady" will be the equivalent of "a young lady pretty" or *una señorita bonita.*

Expect to make mistakes with the rules for agreement of Spanish adjectives and nouns for some time, but don't worry. In most instances your listeners will understand you despite the lack of agreement.

### Possessive Adjectives

Possessive adjectives are those special adjectives that are equivalent to our words "my," "her," "their," "our" and so forth. They are as follows:

| Singular | | Plural | |
|---|---|---|---|
| mi | my | mis | my |
| su | his; her; your | sus | their; your |
| nuestro | our (*m.*) | nuestros | our (*m.*) |
| nuestra | our (*f.*) | nuestras | our (*f.*) |

The important point to know is that possessive adjectives agree with the thing possessed rather than with the possessor. Therefore, "my keys" is not *mi llaves* but rather *mis llaves* as *llaves* is the thing possessed and is plural.

## Present Tense of Regular -er and -ir Verbs

You learned the endings for the present tense of regular -*ar* verbs in Lesson 1 and they constitute the largest of the three conjugations of Spanish verbs. However, there are many verbs that fall into the categories of -*er* and -*ir* verbs.

The following are examples of the -*er* verb forms:

*comer* (to eat)

| | |
|---|---|
| yo como | I eat |
| él/ella/usted come | he/she/you (*for.*) eat(s) |
| nosotros/-as comemos | we eat |
| ellos/ellas/ustedes comen | they/you (*pl.*) eat |

Common -*er* verbs that follow the same pattern as the above include:

| | |
|---|---|
| comprender | to understand |
| vender | to sell |
| beber | to drink |
| creer | to believe |
| leer | to read |

The following are examples of the -*ir* verb forms:

*subir* (to take up, to come up)

|  |  |
|---|---|
| yo subo | I take up |
| él/ella/usted sube | he/she/you (*for.*) take(s) up |
| nosotros/-as subimos | we take up |
| ellos/ellas/ustedes suben | they/you (*pl.*) take up |

Common -*ir* verbs that follow the same pattern include:

|  |  |
|---|---|
| recibir | to receive |
| escribir | to write |
| vivir | to live |
| insistir | to insist |
| decidir | to decide |

## The Irregular Verb **ir**

A good number of the most commonly used verbs in Spanish are highly irregular and in a number of tenses must simply be memorized. The good news is that in a few cases a little memorization can go a long way. One of these cases is the use of the verb "to go," or *ir*, in a structure that serves well as a substitute for the future tense. You must, however, first learn the present tense of *ir* which is as follows:

|  |  |
|---|---|
| yo voy | I go, I'm going |
| él/ella/usted va | he/she goes, you (*for.*) go |
|  | he's/she's/you're going |
| nosotros/-as vamos | we go, we're going |
| ellos/ellas/ustedes van | they/you (*pl.*) go |
|  | they're/you're (*pl.*) going |

## Ir a + *Infinitive*

To form the substitute for the future tense, choose the appropriate form of *ir* and follow it with the preposition *a* plus an infinitive. For example:

*Vamos a comer en el hotel mañana.*
We are going to eat in the hotel tomorrow.

*Va a llegar a México pronto.*
He is going to arrive in Mexico soon.

The "we" form *vamos* when followed by the preposition *a* and an infinitive means "We are going to + (verb)." But it has another meaning as well. It's the way to express the concept of "Let's." Thus, *Vamos a comer en el hotel* can mean "We are going to eat in the hotel" or "Let's eat in the hotel."

## Hay

A most useful irregular Spanish verb is the little word *hay*. It means "there is" or "there are." Happily it has no subject and does not change form:

*Hay una lavandería en el hotel.*
There's a laundry in the hotel.

*Hay otros servicios en el hotel.*
There are other services in the hotel.

It can also be used in questions:

> *¿Hay una lavandería en el hotel?*
> Is there a laundry in the hotel?

> *¿Hay otros servicios en el hotel?*
> Are there other services in the hotel?

## Hay que + *Infinitive*

A very useful idiom using the word *hay* is *hay que* + infinitive. This structure is used to express an impersonal obligation. It is equivalent to the English "one must/has to," "it's necessary to," "you must," and "people must." Example:

> *Hay que pasar por la aduana en el aeropuerto.*
> One must pass through customs in the airport.

It can be used as a question as well:

> *¿Hay que pasar por la aduana en el aeropuerto?*
> Must one pass through customs in the airport?

# Exercises

I.   Fill in the blanks with the correct form of *ser*:

1. El gusto _____ mío.

2. Nosotros _____ socios.

3. Qué bonito _____ el aeropuerto.

4. El señor Sandoval _____ hombre de negocios.

5. Ellos _____ mexicanos.

6. Yo _____ Luisa Vega.

II.  Express in Spanish:

1. Luisa's suitcase

2. the hotel's restaurant

3. Mr. Ortega's trip

4. Jorge's luggage

5. customs' system

III. Express in Spanish:

1. the pretty room

2. the kind gentleman

3. the double bed

4. the red light

5. a good hotel

6. a great man

IV.  Fill in the blanks with the correct possessive adjectives:

1. (my) _____ maleta

2. (our) _____ hotel

3. (their) _____ taxi

4. (her) _____ habitación

5. (your *pl.*) _____ reservaciones

V.  Give the correct form of the following regular -*er* and -*ir* verbs in agreement with the subject pronoun cues:

1. yo:  subir, comer, vivir

2. él:  leer, abrir, comprender

3. ellas:  escribir, subir, vender

4. nosotros:  creer, abrir, vivir

5. ustedes:  beber, comer, recibir

VI.  Fill in the blanks with the correct forms of *ir*:

1. Yo_____ a Cuba.

2. Nosotros _____ al hotel.

3. Mis socios _____ al aeropuerto.

4. Ellos _____ al restaurante.

5. Ustedes _____ en taxi.

6. Ella _____ al salón de belleza y él _____ a la barbería.

VII. Change the following to convey a future idea by using *ir a* + infinitive:

1. Ellos <u>comen</u> en el restaurante.

2. Nosotros <u>pasamos</u> por la aduana.

3. El botones <u>sube</u> el equipaje.

4. Jorge <u>reclama</u> la maleta.

5. El señor Sandoval <u>presenta</u> a su socio al señor Dávila.

VIII. Answer the following questions:

1. ¿Hay servicio a la habitación en el hotel?

2. ¿Hay otros servicios en el hotel?

3. ¿No hay cama matrimonial en la habitación?

4. ¿Hay restaurante en el aeropuerto?

5. ¿Hay habitaciones dobles en el hotel Meliá Habana?

6. ¿Hay que comer en el restaurante del hotel?

## Word Study

There are two verbs in Spanish that mean "to take," but they are not interchangeable. *Llevar* means "to take someone or something from one place to another." *Tomar* means "to take" in the sense of "to pick something up." It is also used in the context of "to take a train, bus or plane," etc. Still another meaning of *tomar* is "to take something to eat or drink." Examples:

*Voy a llevar a mi mamá a casa.*
I'm going to take mother home.

*Rafael toma el boleto de la mesa.*
Rafael picks up the ticket from the table.

*Va a tomar el tren para Lima mañana.*
He's going to take the train for Lima tomorrow.

*Ellos siempre toman café por la mañana.*
They always drink coffee in the morning.

## A Few Facts About the Caribbean

In the Americas, the Cubans are the most informal in their use of the formal and informal "you." They say *Nos tuteamos en seguida,* or "We use *tú* immediately." Because of this regional practice they often unintentionally give offense when they travel abroad. Their accent, also, is unmistakable. They are famous for "swallowing their esses," that is, not pronouncing the final *s* on many words. Other Spanish-speaking areas in the Caribbean share this characteristic but nowhere is it more pronounced than in Cuba.

In Cuba, a bus is a *guagua* and a taxi is a *máquina* (machine).

Taste delights not to be missed are *lechón asado* (roast suckling pig) and *frijoles negros con arroz blanco* (black beans and white rice). The latter are also called *moros y cristianos* (Moors and Christians). When white rice is mixed together with black or kidney beans it's called *arroz congrí.*

You answer the phone by saying *¿Qué hay? "*What is there?" or *¿Oigo?,* "I hear."

Though the Spanish-speaking areas of the Caribbean region are so very near one another geographically, there are many differences in language usage. For example, a *guagua* is a bus throughout the region, while the words for "popcorn" are different in all three places—*rositas de maíz* ("little roses of corn") in Cuba; *cocaleka,* a non-Spanish word, in the Dominican Republic; and *palomitas* ("little doves") in Puerto Rico. It's interesting that almost every Spanish-speaking country has its own word for this tasty snack.

If you ever visit the Dominican Republic sample their regional dish *sancocho*, a stew of yucca, plantains and several types of meat. In Puerto Rico, don't miss their *pernil*, roast pork Puerto Rican style, and a side of *arroz con gandules*, rice and pigeon peas. *¡Que le aproveche!* That's "bon appétit" in Spanish.

LESSON

3

# En el Restaurante

## Diálogo

*Ramón García y Pablo Macías, en un viaje de la Argentina a Santiago de Chile para comprar vinos chilenos, salen juntos para comer en un restaurante muy recomendado. Están cansados y tienen hambre:*

**Ramón:** Buenas noches. Tenemos reservación en nombre de Ramón García.

**Waiter:** Sí, como no. ¿Está bien esta mesa?

**Pablo:** ¿Tiene una mesa que no está tan cerca de la cocina?

**Mozo:** Sí, como no. ¿Es mejor esta mesa?

**Pablo:** Sí, está muy bien.

**Mozo:** ¿Qué van a tomar?

**Ramón:** Me imagino que debemos tomar uno de los vinos chilenos tan excelentes, pero yo tengo ganas de tomar cerveza esta noche. Traígame una botella de Royal Guard, por favor.

**Pablo:** Voy a tomar una copa de vino Santa Carolina. Es mi favorito.

*Estudian el menú:*

**Ramón:** Tienen un menú muy completo aquí. No puedo decidir si quiero carne, ave o pescado. Todo parece delicioso y yo tengo mucha hambre.

# In the Restaurant

## Dialogue

*Ramón García and Pablo Macías, on a trip from Argentina to Santiago de Chile to buy Chilean wines, go out together to eat in a highly recommended restaurant. They're tired and hungry:*

**Ramón:** Good evening. We have a reservation in the name of Ramón García.

**Waiter:** Yes indeed. Is this table satisfactory?

**Pablo:** Do you have a table that's not so close to the kitchen?

**Waiter:** Certainly. Is this table better?

**Pablo:** Yes, this is fine.

**Waiter:** What would you like to drink?

**Ramón:** I imagine we should drink some of that excellent Chilean wine, but I feel like drinking beer tonight. Bring me a bottle of Royal Guard, please.

**Pablo:** I'm going to have a glass of Santa Carolina wine. It's my favorite.

*Studying the menu:*

**Ramón:** They certainly have a very complete menu here. I can't decide whether I want meat, poultry or fish. It all looks good and I'm hungry.

**Mozo:** ¿Están listos para ordenar?

**Pablo:** Creo que voy a pedir pollo frito y una ensalada.

**Ramón:** (al mozo) ¿Qué recomienda usted?

**Mozo:** Quizás nuestro plato regional, pastel de choclo. Es un guisado de choclo, carne de res molida, pollo, pasas, cebollas y huevos duros. Es muy popular en Chile.

**Ramón:** Está bien. Voy a probar eso. Y traígame otra cerveza, por favor.

*Ramón y Pablo comen sus platos fuertes y después el mozo les pregunta:*

**Mozo:** ¿Les gustarían postre y café?

**Pablo:** Me gustaría helado de chocolate, pero no quiero café.

**Ramón:** Ningún postre para mí, gracias. Pero me puede traer otra botella de esa buena cerveza.

*Pablo pide la cuenta:*

**Pablo:** La cuenta, por favor.

**Ramón:** Ay sí, señor. ¿Y dónde está el servicio de hombres? ¡Es urgente!

**Waiter:** Are you ready to order, gentlemen?

**Pablo:** I think I'm going to have fried chicken and a salad.

**Ramón:** (to the waiter) What do you recommend?

**Waiter:** Perhaps our popular regional dish, *pastel de choclo.* It's a casserole of corn, ground beef, chicken, raisins, onions and hard-boiled eggs. It's very popular in Chile.

**Ramón:** OK. I'll try that. And bring me another beer, please.

*They finish the entrée and the waiter asks:*

**Waiter:** Would you like dessert and coffee?

**Pablo:** I'd like some chocolate ice cream, but no coffee.

**Ramón:** No dessert for me, thanks. But I will have another bottle of that good beer.

*Pablo calls for the bill:*

**Pablo:** Bring us the bill, please.

**Ramón:** Oh yes, and waiter, where's the men's room? It's urgent!

## *Vocabulary*

| | |
|---|---|
| a | to |
| aquí | here |
| ave | poultry |
| botella | bottle |
| buena | good |
| café | coffee |
| cansados | tired |
| carne | meat |
| cebollas | onions |
| cerveza | beer |
| chileno | Chilean |
| choclo | corn (*Chi.*) |
| completo | complete |
| comprar | to buy |
| copa | (wine) glass |
| creo | I believe |
| cuenta | bill, check |
| de | from |
| debemos | we ought |
| decidir | to decide |
| delicioso | delicious |
| duros | hard-boiled |
| ensalada | salad |
| es | it's |
| ¿es? | is? |
| esa | that (*f.*) |
| esta | this (*f.*) |
| están | they are |
| ¿están? | are you? |
| esto | this (*n.*) |
| excelentes | excellent |
| favorito | favorite |

| ganas | an urge |
| hambre | hunger |
| helado de chocolate | chocolate ice cream |
| huevos | eggs |
| ¿les gustarían? | would you (*pl.*) like? |
| listos | ready |
| me imagino | I imagine |
| mejor | better |
| menú | menu |
| mesa | table |
| mí | me |
| mi | my |
| molida | ground |
| mozo | waiter |
| muy | very |
| ningún | no |
| noche | night |
| nombre | name |
| nuestro | our |
| o | or |
| ordenar | to order |
| otra | another |
| para | in order to |
| parece | seems |
| pasas | raisins |
| pastel de choclo | corn casserole |
| pedir | to ask for |
| pero | but |
| pescado | fish |
| pide | he asks for |
| plato fuerte | main course |
| pollo frito | fried chicken |
| popular | popular |
| postre | dessert |

| | |
|---|---|
| pregunta | asks |
| probar | to try |
| puedo | I can |
| que | that |
| ¿qué? | what? |
| quiero | I want |
| quizás | perhaps |
| recomendado | recommended |
| ¿recomienda usted? | do you recommend? |
| res | beef |
| reservación | reservation |
| restaurante | restaurant |
| salen | they go out |
| si | if |
| tan | so |
| tenemos | we have |
| tengo | I have |
| terminan | they finish |
| tienen | they have |
| tienen hambre | they're hungry |
| todo | everything |
| tomar | to drink |
| traígame | bring me |
| uno | one |
| ¿van? | are you going? |
| vino | wine |
| voy | I'm going |
| y | and |

## Expressions

| | |
|---|---|
| Está bien. | OK. |
| Sí, como no. | Yes, of course. |

# Grammar

## The Verb estar, "to be"

It seems to be a given in most languages that the most common verbs usually are the most irregular. The verb *ser,* one of the two verbs that mean "to be" in Spanish, was introduced in Lesson 2.

The verb *estar,* "to be," is used principally in two ways:

1) To indicate location as in "Ramón is in the restaurant," *Ramón está en el restaurante* or "Valparaíso is in Chile," *Valparaíso está en Chile.*

2) When followed by an adjective to describe a passing condition rather than a permanent trait. *¿Cómo está usted? Estoy muy bien, gracias.* "How are you? I'm very well, thanks." (That's how the person is feeling now. However, he or she may get sick tomorrow.) *Ramón está cansado.* "Ramón is tired." (We hope that Ramón will be rested tomorrow after a good night's sleep.)

The following are the present tense forms of *estar:*

| | |
|---|---|
| yo estoy | I am |
| él/ella/usted está | he/she is, you (*for.*) are |
| nosotros/-as estamos | we are |
| ellos/ellas/ustedes están | they/you (*pl.*) are |

## The Present Progressive Tense

*Estar* is also the helping verb that is used to form the present progressive tense. In contrast to the simple present tense, the present progressive tense stresses the action in progress. Just as in English we say, "I eat" (the simple present) we also say "I am eating" (the present progressive).

In Spanish, the latter tense is formed by combining the present tense form of *estar* and the present participle of the appropriate verb.

The present participle is the equivalent of the English *-ing* form of the verb. In Spanish, the present participle is formed by dropping the *-ar* ending of the infinitive and adding *-ando* and dropping the *-er* and *-ir* endings and adding *-iendo*. It is as follows:

| Infinitive | Present participle |
|---|---|
| viajar | viajando |
| comer | comiendo |
| vivir | viviendo |

Thus, "Are you talking to your partner on the phone?" "No, I'm calling Mr. Dávila," is *¿Está hablando con su socio por teléfono? No, estoy llamando al señor Dávila.* This present tense form is quite easy to master and very useful.

There are, of course, a few irregular present participles that just have to be learned. Among the more common are:

| | |
|---|---|
| decir (to say or to tell) | diciendo (saying) |
| dormir (to sleep) | durmiendo (sleeping) |

leer (to read)                     leyendo (reading)
pedir (to ask for, to order)       pidiendo (asking for, ordering)

## The Irregular Verbs venir and tener

The verbs *venir*, "to come," and *tener*, "to have," follow a similar pattern in the present tense, as follows:

*venir* (to come)

| | |
|---|---|
| yo vengo | I come |
| él/ella/usted viene | he/she comes, you (*for.*) come |
| nosotros/-as venimos | we come |
| ellos/ellas/ustedes vienen | they/you (*pl.*) come |

*tener* (to have)

| | |
|---|---|
| yo tengo | I have |
| él/ella/usted tiene | he/she has, you (*for.*) have |
| nosotros/-as tenemos | we have |
| ellos/ellas/ustedes tienen | they/you (*pl.*) have |

Note that the "we" form is the only form that differs between the two verbs. This is because *venir* is an *-ir* verb and *tener* is an *-er* verb.

## Uses of tener

The verb *tener* is only used to mean "to have" in the sense of "to possess." It's a very useful verb in that it is the basis of a series of common idioms.

By using the conjugated form of *tener* + *que* followed by the infinitive of a verb you convey the idea of "having to do something." For example, "Ramón and Carlos have to eat in a restaurant." *Ramón y Carlos tienen que comer en un restaurante.* "We have to go to Chile." *Tenemos que ir a Chile.* A number of other useful expressions are formed with *tener* followed by a noun. You'll remember from Part 2 of Getting Started that age, for example, is told by saying "I have (so many) years," *Tengo _____ años.*

Other common idiomatic expressions based on the verb *tener* include the concepts of hunger, thirst, cold, heat, being right or wrong, etc. In these cases what is being said literally is "I have hunger," "He has heat," "Julio has reason (on his side)," "He has cold." Among the more common of these idioms are:

| | |
|---|---|
| tener hambre | to be hungry |
| tener sed | to be thirsty |
| tener calor | to be hot |
| tener razón | to be right (have reason on one's side) |
| no tener razón | to be wrong (not have reason on one's side) |
| tener miedo | to be afraid |
| tener frío | to be cold |
| tener ganas (de) | to have a desire to, to feel like |
| tener cuidado | to be careful (to have care) |

## The Personal a

A detail in Spanish that has no equivalent in English is the use of what is called the personal *a*.

This preposition is used before a direct object that is a person. Example: "Ramón invites Carlos to eat in a restaurant." *Ramón invita a Carlos a comer en un restaurante.* There is one exception. The personal *a* is generally not used with the verb *tener.* Example: "He has two partners." *El tiene dos socios.*

If the direct object is not a person, the personal *a* is not normally used.

Animal lovers will be happy to know that when a pet is considered a member of the family, it usually rates a personal *a*.

## Contractions

There are only two contractions in Spanish: *al* and *del*.

The preposition *a* when followed by *el* contracts to *al*.
Example: *Vamos al restaurante.*

The preposition *de* when followed by *el* contracts to *del*.
Example: *Vienen del aeropuerto.*

## Exercises

I.  Change the following sentences using the words in parentheses. You may also have to change the adjectives to agree appropriately:

1. Ellos están bien. (Yo)

2. El está listo. (Marta)

3. El pastel de choclo está delicioso hoy. (La carne)

4. Nosotros no estamos bien. (Ellos)

5. Julia está cansada. (Julio)

II. Change the following infinitives to the present participle, or -ing form of the verb:

1. hablar            _____

2. decir             _____

3. decidir           _____

4. pedir             _____

5. vivir             _____

6. conocer           _____

III. Complete the following sentences using the present progressive form of the verbs in parentheses:

1. El mozo (servir) _____ el pollo.

2. Yo (escribir) _____ ahora.

3. Ellos (comer) _____ en un restaurante excelente.

4. El botones (subir) _____ el equipaje a la habitación.

5. Nosotras (tomar) _____ una copa de vino.

IV. Fill in the blanks with the correct form of the infinitive in parentheses:

1. Nosotros (tener) _____ que presentar los papeles.

2. Yo (venir) _____ de Santiago de Chile.

3. Ellos (venir) _____ para comprar vino.

4. Ella (tener) _____ dos maletas.

5. Yo (tener) _____ miedo.

V. Express the following in Spanish:

1. She has to buy Chilean wine.

2. I have to go to the airport.

3. Do we have to eat in that restaurant?

4. Ramón and Pablo have to wait for dessert.

5. Jorge and Luisa have to have a double bed. They're newlyweds.

VI. Fill in the blank with the personal *a* where required:

1. No tengo _____ amigos.

2. Comen _____ carne.

3. Quiero presentarle _____ un socio mío.

4. ¿Buscamos _____ Jorge?

5. Voy a pedir _____ pollo frito.

VII. Fill in the blanks with one of the following: *de la, de las, del, de los, a la, a las, al, a los:*

1. El señor Macías es amigo _____ señor García.

2. La cerveza _____ restaurante es deliciosa.

3. Tenemos el número de teléfono _____ señora Martínez.

4. El vino es _____ amigo de Carlos.

5. Vamos _____ aeropuerto.

6. El equipaje _____ señoras está en la habitación.

## Word Study

The meaning of an adjective can change, sometimes dramatically, depending on whether it follows the verb *ser* or the verb *estar*. Examples:

*La mujer es pálida.*
The woman is pale-complexioned.
*La mujer está pálida hoy.*
The woman looks pale today.

*La niña es mala.*
The girl is bad.
*La niña está mala.*
The girl is sick.

*Rosa es buena.*
Rosa is a good woman.
*Rosa está buena.*
She's really built. (Often accompanied by the gesture of two hands outlining the female body.)

*Daniel es listo.*
Daniel is a smart guy.
*Daniel está listo.*
Daniel is ready.

*Cómo es el señor Vega?*
What's Mr. Vega like? (Calls for a description.)
*Cómo está el señor Vega?*
How's Mr. Vega's health?

## A Few Facts About Chile

The names of food often differ from one country to another. In this respect Chile tends to share its usage with the other southern South American countries, a region often referred to as the "Cone" of South America. These words include the word *palta* for "avocado" for example.

McDonald's in Santiago de Chile offers on its menu a McPalta burger. Also in Chile, corn is known as *choclo*. In most parts of the Spanish-speaking world an avocado is called *aguacate* and corn is *maíz*.

An interesting language detail about Chile is that the afternoon tea is called *las onces*. One would think that "elevenses" would be eaten at II:00 A.M., but not so. Usage is the same among Chile's Andean neighbors.

Another food (or rather drink) related word is *schopería*. This is what they call the new popular establishments where Chileans go to drink mug beer. The name is a combination of German and Spanish, as there are many Germans in Chile. These places are not unlike English pubs.

Another word that's typically Chilean in its use is the word *guagua*. In the Caribbean a *guagu*a is a bus; in Chile, it's the word for "baby." The story is told, most probably apocryphal, that a Chilean on a trip to Cuba read the following headline in a local paper: *GUAGUA MATA A UN POLICIA* (BUS KILLS POLICEMAN). In amazement, he comments: "This would never happen in my country!"

If you enjoy your "happy hours" be sure to try a *pisco* sour. It's a popular Chilean cocktail not unlike a *margarita*. For the bolder, sample the Chilean *chicha*, a strong alcoholic drink made of grapes left over from the fall harvest.

# LESSON
# 4

# Los Nombres

## Diálogo

*Los señores Vargas de Caracas, Venezuela, están de visita en casa de su hija Cecilia y su yerno Carlos que viven en Maracaibo. La ocasión es el nacimiento reciente de su primera nieta:*

**Carlos:** Bienvenidos a nuestra casa. Están en su casa. ¿Encontraron esta dirección sin problema?

**Abuelo:** Sí, el taxista la encontró sin dificultad.

**Carlos:** Voy a llevar su equipaje al cuarto de huéspedes y entonces podemos cenar. Tengo una buena botella de vino y Cecilia ha preparado una cena maravillosa.

**Abuela:** Basta de conversación. Yo no puedo esperar ni un minuto más para ver a mi nueva nieta.

**Cecilia:** Yo sé, mamá, pero ella acaba de dormirse. Vamos a cenar primero.

**Carlos:** Sí, vamos a tener una pequeña fiesta.

**Abuelo:** Seguro. Yo sé que al menos yo tengo hambre. Era un viaje largo.

**Abuela:** Tu (*fam.*) estómago siempre viene primero ¿verdad?

# Names

## *Dialogue*

*Mr. and Mrs. Vargas, from Caracas, Venezuela, are visiting the home of their daughter Cecilia and their son-in-law Carlos, who live in Maracaibo. The occasion is the recent birth of their first grandchild:*

**Carlos:** Welcome to our house. Please feel at home. Did you have trouble finding this address?

**Granddad:** No, the taxi driver found it with no difficulty.

**Carlos:** I'll take your luggage to the guest room and then we can have some dinner. I've got a good bottle of wine and Cecilia has a wonderful meal ready.

**Grandma:** Enough conversation. I can't wait a minute longer to see my new little granddaughter.

**Cecilia:** I know, mom, but she just went to sleep. Let's have some dinner first.

**Carlos:** Yes, let's have a little celebration.

**Granddad:** Sure. I know I'm hungry. It was a long trip.

**Grandma:** Your stomach always comes first, right?

*Todos se sientan a la mesa:*

**Abuela:** ¡Qué bonita es la mesa! Las flores son muy lindas.

**Carlos:** Y con esta deliciosa *hallaca* venezolana y un excelente vino chileno éste sí va a ser un verdadero banquete.

*Después de la comida:*

**Abuela:** Vamos a comer el postre después. Ya es hora de ver a esa bebé.

*En el cuarto de la bebé:*

**Abuela:** ¡Es preciosa! ¿Ya han escogido ustedes su nombre?

**Cecilia:** Sí. Le pusimos Cecilia por mí, Rosa por tía Rosa, Elena por tía Elena, Leonor por tía Leonor, Olivia por tía Olivia y Dora por tía Dora.

**Abuela:** ¿Y por mí, nada?

**Cecilia:** Ay sí, por supuesto. Y María por ti (*fam.*).

**Abuelo:** ¿Entonces ella se llama Cecilia Rosa Elena Leonor Olivia Dora María Vargas Martín? ¡Qué nombre tan largo para una niña tan pequeña!

**Cecilia:** No hay problema. Vamos a llamarla sencillamente Ceci.

*They all sit down at the table:*

**Grandma:** How beautiful the table looks! The flowers are lovely.

**Granddad:** And with a delicious Venezuelan *hallaca* and an excellent Chilean wine this really is a celebration.

*After the main course:*

**Grandma:** Let's have dessert later. It's time to see that baby.

*In the baby's room:*

**Grandma:** She's precious. Have you decided on her name?

**Cecilia:** Yes. She's going to be Cecilia after me, Rosa after Aunt Rosa, Elena after Aunt Elena, Leonor after Aunt Leonor, Olivia after Aunt Olivia and Dora after Aunt Dora.

**Grandma:** And what about me?

**Cecilia:** Oh, yes, of course. And María after you.

**Granddad:** So she's going to be Cecilia Rosa Elena Leonor Olivia Dora María Vargas Martín? What a long name for such a little girl!

**Cecilia:** That's no problem. We're just going to call her Ceci.

## Vocabulary

| | |
|---|---|
| abuela | grandmother |
| abuelo | grandfather |
| acaba de | she has just |
| ay sí | oh, yes |
| basta de | enough |
| bebé | baby (*m. or f.*) |
| bienvenidos | welcome |
| botella | bottle |
| celebración | celebration |
| cenar | to eat dinner |
| chica | little |
| conversación | conversation |
| cuarto | room |
| después de | after |
| dificultad | difficulty |
| dirección | address |
| dormir(se) | to go to sleep |
| el taxista | taxi driver |
| en encontrar | in finding |
| entonces | then |
| era | it was |
| esa | that |
| esperar | to wait |
| esta | this |
| están visitando | they are visiting |
| estómago | stomach |
| flores | flowers |

| | |
|---|---|
| hallaca | (mixture of cornmeal with meat, peppers, raisins, olives, onions and spices, wrapped in banana leaves and boiled) |
| han escogido | you have chosen |
| hija | daughter |
| hora | time |
| huésped | guest |
| lo/la encontró | he/she/it found it |
| largo | long |
| lindas | pretty |
| llamarla | to call her |
| llevar | to take |
| maravillosa | marvelous |
| más | more |
| nacimiento | birth |
| nada | nothing |
| nieta | granddaughter |
| niña | girl |
| nombre | name |
| nueva | new |
| ocasión | occasion |
| para | for, in order to |
| pequeña | little |
| podemos | we can |
| por | for |
| postre | dessert |
| preciosa | precious |
| preparada | prepared |

| primera | first  (f.) |
|---|---|
| primero | first (m.) |
| problema | problem |
| puedo | I can |
| pues | well |
| que | that |
| ¡qué—! | what a—! |
| reciente | recent |
| se sientan | they sit down |
| seguro | sure |
| sencillamente | simply |
| sin | without |
| tan | so |
| ¿tenían? | did you have? |
| tía | aunt |
| todos | everyone |
| venezolana | Venezuelan (f.) |
| ver | to see |
| verdadera | real |
| ya | now, already |
| yo sé | I know |

## *Expressions*

| Están en su casa. | Feel right at home. (pl.) (literally: You are in your house.) |
|---|---|
| Por supuesto. | Of course. |

# Grammar

## *Formation of Adverbs*

Many adverbs in Spanish end in *–mente* which is like the "ly" in English. The *-mente* ending is added to the feminine singular form of the adjective. Thus the word *lento* meaning "slow" becomes the adverb *lentamente* or "slowly." There are, however, many adverbs that do not end in *-mente* and simply must be learned as individual vocabulary. For example, there's another adverb in Spanish that also means "slowly," *despacio.*

## *Comparison of Adjectives and Adverbs—Regular Forms*

Comparisons of inequality of most adjectives and adverbs are formed by putting either the word *más* (more) or *menos* (less) before the adjective or adverb and following it with the word *que*, as follows:

*más*     +   (adjective or adverb)   +   *que*
*menos*  +   (adjective or adverb)   +   *que*

*Este viaje es más largo que el viaje a Caracas.*
This trip is longer than the trip to Caracas.

*Abuela come menos que abuelo.*
Grandmother eats less than grandfather.

To form comparisons of equality with nouns and pronouns, adjectives and adverbs, use the adjective *tanto* or the adverb *tan*, plus *como*: *tanto ... como* "as much ... as" or *tan ... como* "as ... as."  As *tanto* is an adjective it must agree in gender and number with the noun it modifies (*tanto, tantos, tanta, tantas*). Examples:

> *El tiene tanto dinero como ella.*
> He has as much money as she (does).

> *Abuela viaja tan fácilmente como abuelo.*
> Grandmother travels as easily as grandfather.

## Comparison of Adjectives—Irregular Forms

Some adjectives are irregular in their comparative forms. The most common are the following:

| Adjective | | Comparative | | Superlative | |
|---|---|---|---|---|---|
| bueno | good | mejor | better | el mejor | the best |
| malo | bad | peor | worse | el peor | the worst |
| viego | old | mayor | older | el mayor | the oldest |
| pequeño | young | menor | younger | el menor | the youngest |

*Grande* and *pequeño* also mean "large" and "small." When this is the case, their comparison is regular:

> *Este cuarto es más grande que la habitación en el hotel.*
> This room is larger than the room in the hotel.

> *La niña es más pequeña que su hermana.*
> The girl is smaller than her sister.

## Superlatives

The superlative of an adjective is formed by putting the appropriate definite article before the noun being compared, then adding either *más* (more) or *menos* (less) and the adjective. Remember that the article and adjective must agree with the noun. The pattern is as follows:

definite article + noun + *más* or *menos* + adjective

Examples:

la comida más deliciosa     the most delicious meal
los cuartos menos cómodos   the least comfortable rooms

After a superlative in Spanish the preposition *de* translates the English preposition "in":

> *Es el hombre más inteligente de esta ciudad.*
> He's the most intelligent man in this city.

## Present Tense of e to ie Stem-Changing Verbs

Some Spanish verbs have a stem change from *e* to *ie* and from *o* to *ue* in the present tense. This change occurs in all but the "we" form of the present tense Such a change occurs, for example, in the -ar verb *cerrar* (to close), the -er verb *querer* (to wish, to want) and the -ir verb *preferir* (to prefer).

The present tense conjugations of these three verbs are as follows:

*cerrar* (to close)

| | |
|---|---|
| yo cierro | I close |
| él/ella/usted cierra | he/she closes, you (*for.*) close |
| nosotros/-as cerramos | we close |
| ellos/ellas/ustedes cierran | they/you (*pl.*) close |

*querer* (to wish, to want)

| | |
|---|---|
| yo quiero | I want |
| él/ella/usted quiere | he/she wants, you (*for.*) want |
| nosotros/-as queremos | we want |
| ellos/ellas/ustedes quieren | they/you (*pl.*) want |

*preferir* (to prefer)

| | |
|---|---|
| yo prefiero | I prefer |
| él/ella/usted prefiere | he/she prefers, you (*for.*) prefer |
| nosotros/-as preferimos | we prefer |
| ellos/ellas/ustedes prefieren | they/you (*pl.*) prefer |

Other common verbs of this type include:

*-ar* verbs

| | |
|---|---|
| empezar | to begin |
| comenzar | to begin |
| pensar | to think |

*-er* verbs

| | |
|---|---|
| entender | to understand |
| perder | to lose |

*-ir* verbs

| | |
|---|---|
| sugerir | to suggest |
| mentir | to lie |
| convertir | to convert |

## Present Tense of o to ue Stem-changing Verbs

Verbs whose stems change from *o* to *ue* in the present tense include the *-ar* verb *encontrar* (to find, to meet), the *-er* verb *poder* (to be able, can) and the *-ir* verb *dormir* (to sleep). Their present tense conjugations are as follows:

*encontrar* (to find, to meet)

| | |
|---|---|
| yo encuentro | I find |
| él/ella/usted encuentra | he/she finds, |
| | you (*for.*) find |
| nosotros/-as encontramos | we find |
| ellos/ellas/ustedes encuentran | they/you (*pl.*) find |

*poder* (to be able, can)

| | |
|---|---|
| yo puedo | I can |
| él/ella/usted puede | he/she/you (*for.*) can |
| nosotros/-as podemos | we can |
| ellos/ellas/ustedes pueden | they/you (*pl.*) can |

*dormir* (to sleep)

| | |
|---|---|
| yo duermo | I sleep |
| él/ella/usted duerme | he/she sleeps, you (*for.*) sleep |
| nosotros/-as dormimos | we sleep |
| ellos/ellas/ustedes duermen | they/you (*pl.*) sleep |

Other common verbs of this type include:

*-ar* verbs

| | |
|---|---|
| contar | to count |
| costar | to cost |
| probar | to try |
| recordar | to remember |

*-er* verbs

| | |
|---|---|
| llover | to rain |
| resolver | to resolve |
| mover | to move |

*-ir* verb

| | |
|---|---|
| morir | to die |

The verb *jugar*, "to play (a game)" has a stem change from _u_ to _ue_ in the same persons and numbers as the above. Its present tense conjugation is as follows:

| | |
|---|---|
| yo juego | I play |
| él/ella/usted juega | he/she plays, you (*for.*) play |

| | |
|---|---|
| nosotros/-as jugamos | we play |
| ellos/ellas/ustedes juegan | they/you (*pl.*) play |

## Weather Expressions

In Spanish, the verb *hacer* ("to do" or "to make") is usually used to describe the weather. So instead of saying "It's cold," Spanish speakers literally say "It makes (*hace*) cold." Note the following weather expressions:

| | |
|---|---|
| Hace frío. | It's cold. |
| Hace calor. | It's hot. |
| Hace viento. | It's windy. |
| Hace sol. | It's sunny. |

As *frío, calor, viento* and *sol* are actually the nouns "cold, heat, wind and sun" you must use the adjective *mucho* to convey the idea of "very." Thus *Hace mucho frío* (literally, "It makes much cold") is equivalent to the English "It's very cold."

It's also possible to use the word *hay* in weather expressions, as follows:

| | |
|---|---|
| Hay (mucho) frío. | It's (very) cold. |
| Hay (mucho) calor. | It's (very) hot. |
| Hay (mucho) viento. | It's (very) windy. |
| Hay (mucho) sol. | It's (very) sunny. |

To inquire as to the weather in general you say:

*¿Qué tiempo hace hoy?*
How's the weather today?

Appropriate replies would be:

*Hace buen tiempo.*
The weather's good.

*Hace mal tiempo.*
The weather's bad.

*Hace frío.*
It's cold.

*Hace calor.*
It's hot.

To say "It's raining" use the third person singular present tense form of the *o* to *ue* stem-changing verb *llover. Llueve.* To say "It's snowing" use the third person singular present tense form of the *e* to *ie* stem-changing verb *nevar. Nieva.*

## Question Words

Many questions in Spanish begin with special interrogative words. The most frequently used interrogative words are the following:

| | |
|---|---|
| ¿adónde? | (to) where? |
| ¿cómo? | how? |
| ¿cuál(es)? | which one/ones, what? |
| ¿cuándo? | when? |
| ¿cuánto/a? | how much? |
| ¿cuántos/as? | how many? |

| | |
|---|---|
| ¿dónde? | where? |
| ¿qué? | what? |
| ¿quién/es? | who, whom? |

Note that these interrogative words always bear an accent over the stressed syllable. This identifies them as interrogatives.

## Exercises

I.  Change the following adjectives to adverbs:

    1. completo            _____

    2. amable              _____

    3. lento                _____

    4. necesario          _____

    5. cómodo             _____

II.  Express the following in Spanish:

    1. Grandfather is hungrier than grandmother.

    2. My son-in-law is 24 years old and my daughter is 22. Who is the older?

    3. I have a lot of (much) money, but you have more than I (do).

    4. The baby is the prettiest baby in Venezuela.

    5. Juan always comes as late as Leonor.

    6. It's the most comfortable room in the hotel.

III.  Fill in the blanks with the appropriate form of the following stem-changing verbs:

    1. Yo (querer) _____ una botella de cerveza.

    2. La bebé (dormir) _____ mucho.

    3. Ella (preferir) _____ el nombre de Cecilia.

4. Ellos (poder) _____ comer en la casa de su hija y su yerno.

5. Pedro (querer) _____ pollo frito.

6. Mis abuelos (dormir) _____ en el cuarto de huéspedes.

7. Tenemos que (cerrar) _____ las maletas.

8. Yo (preferir) _____ tomar vino esta noche.

IV. Express the following in Spanish:

1. Is it going to snow tomorrow?

2. What's the weather like in Maracaibo?

3. It's very hot.

4. It doesn't snow in Cuba.

5. It's not windy today.

6. It's sunny.

V. Answer the following questions in Spanish:

1. ¿Cómo está usted?

2. ¿Dónde está Caracas?

3. ¿Quién es la mamá de la bebé?

4. ¿Qué hora es? (1:20)

5. ¿Cuánto es el vino? (15 *bolívares*, currency of Venezuela)

6. ¿Cuántos nietos tienen los abuelos?

## Word Study

Cognates are words that are the same or similar in English and Spanish. As there are innumerable such words, it makes vocabulary building much easier. There are, however, a good number of false cognates, Spanish words that look similar to the English, but have different meanings. The following are a few examples:

*asistir* to attend, not to assist

*campo* country in the sense of rural area, not camp

*éxito* success, not exit

*firma* signature, not firm

*largo* long, not large

*introducir* insert, not to introduce a person

*particular* private, not particular

And like these, there are many more. However, there are ever so many other cognates that can be relied upon and that will help students greatly in expanding their vocabularies.

## A Few Facts About Venezuela

Certain words in common usage in Venezuela reflect the influence of English. For example, "tape"—which in most Spanish-speaking countries is *cinta*—is often called *teipe* here. Both city and intercity buses are *autobuses*. And when you go to buy a "ticket" to somewhere you'll hear it called a *tique* as well as the more standard word *boleto*.

Answer the phone by saying, "*Haló.*" This is the most common way of answering the telephone in Latin America so you can't go wrong by using it. Remember that the *H* is silent. There are, of course, a number of possible variations, which are included in other lessons in this book.

If you need to buy razor blades in Venezuela, ask for *gillettes*. This popular brand has come to be used as the general word for "razor blades" here. (Remember when a lot of English-speaking people referred to all refrigerators as Frigidaires?)

The word *bebé* is commonly used for "baby" in Venezuela as in most Spanish-speaking countries, but a baby there is also called a *chamito*.

---

The system of names in Venezuela is the same as it is throughout the Spanish-speaking world. A person's name has a minimum of three parts. The *nombre* is the first, or given, name, such as *Juan, Rosa, Carlos,* etc. The *primer apellido,* or first last name, is the father's family name. The *segundo apellido*, or second last name, is the mother's family name.

Whenever you need to consult any alphabetized list of names, such as the phone directory, you need to look under the first last name as the father's family name is deemed the more important.

When a woman marries, the husband's father's family name is added to her name preceded by the preposition *de*. Thus when María Pérez González marries Pedro García Torres her legal name becomes María Pérez González de García. Fortunately, in actual usage she will usually be called by her maiden name, which in this case would simply be María Pérez.

When a baby is born, the parents often honor other members of the family by giving their names to the child as middle names. Again, in practice these names are rarely used. It is not uncommon in Latin America for a girl to be named for her mother.

LESSON

5

# Visitando los Sitios de Interés

*Diálogo*

*Javier y Francisco son miembros del equipo chileno de fútbol que están en La Paz, Bolivia, para competir. Su juego es el próximo día y ellos están aprovechando esta tarde para ver los sitios de interés en la capital boliviana.*

**Javier:** No puedo creer que La Paz está situada más de tres kilómetros y medio arriba del nivel del mar. Dicen que es la capital más alta del mundo.

**Francisco:** Bueno, tengo muchas ganas de ver sus sitios de interés.

**Javier:** Vamos primero al Palacio Presidencial.

**Francisco:** ¿Sabes (*fam.*) dónde está?

**Javier:** No, no tengo el libro de guía conmigo. Está en el hotel. Pero podemos pedirle direcciones a alguién.

**Francisco:** (a un hombre en la calle) ¿Dónde queda el Palacio Presidencial de aquí?

**Hombre en la calle:** Está un poco lejos.

**Javier:** ¿Podemos caminar para allá?

# Sight-seeing

## Dialogue

*Javier and Francisco are members of the Chilean soccer team who are in La Paz, Bolivia, to play a game. Their game is the next day and they are taking advantage of this afternoon to go sight-seeing in the Bolivian capital.*

**Javier:** I can't believe that La Paz is located two and a quarter miles above sea level. They say it's the highest capital in the world.

**Francisco:** Well, I really want to see its important landmarks.

**Javier:** Let's go first to the Presidential Palace.

**Francisco:** Do you know where it is?

**Javier:** No, I don't have the guidebook with me. It's in the hotel. But we can ask someone for directions.

**Francisco:** (to a man in the street) Where is the Presidential Palace from here?

**Man in the street:** It's a little far.

**Javier:** Can we walk there?

**Hombre en la calle:** Sí, pero va a ser como diez cuadras. Caminen ustedes derecho seis cuadras, entonces doblen a la izquierda y sigan más o menos cuatro cuadras más hasta la calle Comercio.

*Javier y Francisco llegan al Palacio Presidencial. Después de ver todo, Javier le dice a Francisco:*

**Javier:** Este es muy impresionante pero quiero ver la catedral también. La catedral aquí en La Paz es una de las catedrales más grandes de América del Sur.

**Francisco:** Está bien, pero yo no sé dónde está.

**Javier:** Siempre podemos pedir direcciones. (a otro hombre en la calle) ¿Puede usted decirnos dónde está la catedral?

**Hombre en la calle:** Está muy cerca. Queda en la próxima cuadra.

*Después de ver los altares lindos de la catedral, Javier le dice a Francisco:*

**Javier:** También me gustaría ver el Mercado de Hechizador hoy.

**Francisco:** Está bien, pero sé que está bastante lejos. Vamos a tomar taxi. Me falta aire a esta altura.

**Javier:** Bueno, si nos falta aire cuando vamos a ver los sitios de interés de La Paz, ¿cómo vamos a ganar nuestro juego de fútbol mañana?

**Man in the street:** Yes, but it's about ten blocks. You go straight ahead for six blocks, then turn left and go about four blocks more.

*Javier and Francisco reach the palace. After seeing everything, Javier says to Francisco:*

**Javier:** This is very impressive, but I want to see the cathedral, too. The cathedral here in La Paz is one of the largest cathedrals in South America.

**Francisco:** OK, but I don't know where it is.

**Javier:** We can always ask for directions. (to a man in the street) Can you tell us where the cathedral is?

**Man in the street:** It's very close by. It's in the next block. You'll see it right away.

*After viewing the cathedral's fine altars, Javier says to Francisco:*

**Javier:** I'd also like to see the Witchdoctor's Market today.

**Francisco:** OK, but I know that it's far. Let's take a taxi. I'm really short of breath at this altitude.

**Javier:** Well, if we get short of breath when we go sight-seeing, how will we win our soccer game tomorrow?

## Vocabulary

| | |
|---|---|
| alguién | someone |
| alta | high |
| altura | altitude |
| América del Sur | South America |
| aquí | here |
| boliviano | Bolivian |
| calle | street |
| caminar | to walk |
| capital | capital |
| catedral | cathedral |
| cerca | near |
| como | like |
| conmigo | with me |
| creer | to believe |
| cuadra | block |
| cuadras | blocks |
| cuarto | quarter |
| deben | you should |
| decirnos | to tell us |
| después de | after |
| dice | he says |
| dicen | they say |
| direcciones | directions |
| doblen | turn |
| ¿dónde queda? | where is? (variation on ¿dónde está?) |
| el próximo día | the next day |
| en seguida | right away |
| entonces | then |
| esta tarde | this afternoon |

| están aprovechando | they're taking advantage |
| fútbol | soccer |
| ganar | to win |
| hasta | to |
| hombre | man |
| hoy | today |
| impresionante | impressive |
| juego | game |
| jugar | to play (a game) |
| kilómetros | kilometers |
| lejos | far |
| libro de guía | guidebook |
| lindos | pretty |
| llegar | to arrive |
| los altares | the altars |
| los sitios de interés | places of interest |
| me falta aire | I'm short of breath (literally, air is lacking to me) |
| me gustaría | I would like |
| Mercado de Hechizador | Witchdoctor's Market |
| miembros | members |
| nivel del mar | sea level |
| no sé | I don't know |
| nos falta aire | we're short of breath (literally, air is lacking to us) |
| Palacio Presidencial | Presidential Palace |
| para allá | to there |
| pedir | to ask for |
| poco | little |
| próxima | next |

| | |
|---|---|
| ¿sabes? | do you know? (*fam.*) |
| sé | I know |
| sigan derecho | go straight |
| situada | located |
| tengo muchas ganas | I have a yearning |
| todo | everything |
| tomar | to take |
| ver | to see |

## Expressions

| | |
|---|---|
| A la derecha. | To the right. |
| A la izquierda. | To the left. |
| Más o menos. | More or less. |

# Grammar

## *Present Tense of* e *to* i *Stem-changing Verbs*

In the last lesson, you learned that certain verbs have stem-changes in the first and third person singular and third person plural present tense. These changes are either *i* to *ie*, *o* to *ue* or *u* to *ue*.

There are also a few -*ir* verbs that have a stem change from *e* to *i* in the same persons and numbers of the present tense. These verbs include *pedir*, "to ask for, request, order" and *servir*, "to serve."

The present tense forms of these verbs are as follows:

*pedir* (to ask for, request, order)

| | |
|---|---|
| yo pido | I ask for |
| él/ella/usted pide | he/she asks for, you (*for.*) ask for |
| nosotros/-as pedimos | we ask for |
| ellos/ellas/ustedes piden | they/you (*pl.*) ask for |

*servir* (to serve)

| | |
|---|---|
| yo sirvo | I serve |
| él/ella/usted sirve | he/she serves, you (*for.*) serve |
| nosotros/-as servimos | we serve |
| ellos/ellas/ustedes sirven | they/you (*pl.*) serve |

Other common verbs of this type include:

| | |
|---|---|
| seguir | to follow, continue |
| conseguir | to get |
| reír | to laugh |
| sonreír | to smile |
| corregir | to correct |
| competir | to compete |

## Pronouns as Objects of Prepositions

An object of a preposition is the noun or pronoun that follows a preposition. For example, in the sentence *Javier va <u>con Francisco</u> para ver la catedral,* "Javier goes <u>with Francisco</u> to see the cathedral," Francisco is the noun object of the preposition "with." However, the noun "Francisco" can be replaced with the pronoun "him." In this case the sentence would read *Javier va <u>con él</u> para ver la catedral,* "Javier goes <u>with him</u> to see the cathedral." In the latter example *con* (with) is the preposition and *él* (him) is the pronoun object of the preposition.

The forms of the pronouns used as the objects of prepositions are as follows:

| *Singular* | | *Plural* | |
|---|---|---|---|
| mí | me | nosotros/-as | us |
| él | him | ellos | them (*m.*) |
| ella | her | ellas | them (*f.*) |
| usted | you (*for.*) | ustedes | you (*pl.*) |

The pronoun form *mí* bears an accent to differentiate it from the possessive pronoun *mi* meaning "my." When *mí* follows the preposition *con* (with), the prepositional phrase becomes *conmigo.*

### Affirmative and Negative Expressions

The following is a chart that compares affirmative and negative expressions in Spanish:

| Affirmative | Negative |
|---|---|
| *alguien* someone, somebody | *nadie* nobody, no one |
| *algo* something, anything | *nada* nothing, not anything |
| *alguno/-a* any, some | *ninguno/-a* no, none, not any |
| *algún* any, some | *ningún* no, not any |
| *siempre* always | *nunca, jamás* never |
| *también* too, also | *tampoco* not either, neither |
| *o . . . o* either . . . or | *ni . . . ni* neither . . . nor |

*Alguno* and *ninguno* drop the *o* before a masculine singular noun. "Some book" would be *algún libro* and "no book" would be *ningún libro.*

Though double negatives are completely unacceptable in English, Spanish often uses more than one negative in a sentence:

Yo no necesito nada.    I don't need anything.

In fact, if a negative expression goes after the verb it is necessary to put the word *no* before the verb as well. If the negative expression is put before the verb *no* is not used.

No tomo taxi nunca.    *or*    Nunca tomo taxi.
I never take a taxi.

## *Direct Object Pronouns*

A direct object is the part of the sentence that receives the action of the verb directly. For example, in the sentence *Ellos ven el Palacio Presidencial,* "They see the Presidential Palace," *Palacio Presidencial* is the direct object of the verb *ven.* However, the noun form of the direct object is often replaced by the shorter pronoun form as in *Ellos lo ven,* or "They see it." These pronoun forms are as follows:

| *Singular* | | *Plural* | |
|---|---|---|---|
| me | me | nos | us |
| lo | him/it/you (*for.*) | los | them/you (*pl.*) |
| la | her/it/you (*for.*) | las | them/you (*pl.*) |

The direct object pronouns are usually placed before the conjugated form of the verb in Spanish. For example:

| Los turistas ven la catedral. | The tourists see the cathedral. |
|---|---|
| Los turistas <u>la</u> ven. | The tourists see it. |

If the sentence is negative, the *no* must go before the direct object pronoun, as follows:

> *Los turistas no ven la catedral.*
> The tourists don't see the cathedral.

> *Los turistas <u>no la</u> ven.*
> The tourists don't see it.

When an infinitive follows the conjugated form of a verb, the direct object pronoun may go before the conjugated form of the verb or after the infinitive and be attached to it. For example:

Podemos verla de aquí.     *or*     La podemos ver de aquí.
We can see it from here.

The same is true with the present progressive tense (present tense form of *estar* + *present participle*). Example:

Los turistas *están mirándola* ahora.
*or*
Los turistas la *están mirando* ahora.
The tourists are looking at it now.

Note: When object pronouns are attached, it may be necessary to add an accent to preserve the original pronunciation of the infinitive or present participle.

## *More Irregular Verbs*

The present tense forms of the irregular verbs *decir* (to say, to tell), *dar* (to give) and *hacer* (to do, to make) are as follows:

*decir* (to say, to tell)

| | |
|---|---|
| yo digo | I say |
| él/ella/usted dice | he/she says, you (*for.*) say |
| nosotros/-as decimos | we say |
| ellos/ellas/ustedes dicen | they/you (*pl.*) say |

*dar* (to give)

| | |
|---|---|
| yo doy | I give |
| él/ella/usted da | he/she gives, you (*for.*) give |

| | |
|---|---|
| nosotros/-as damos | we give |
| ellos/ellas/ustedes dan | they/you (*pl.*) give |

*hacer* (to do, to make)

| | |
|---|---|
| yo hago | I do, make |
| él/ella/usted hace | he/she does, makes, you (*for.*) do, make |
| nosotros/-as hacemos | we do, make |
| ellos/ellas/ustedes hacen | they/you (*pl.*) do, make |

## Hacer *with Time Expressions*

In English, the present perfect or present perfect progressive tense is used to express how long something has been going on. Example:

We have (eaten) (been eating) in that restaurant for a year.

A completely different structure is used in Spanish. It goes as follows:

*Hace* + length of time + *que* + present tense of verb.

> *¿Hace cuánto tiempo que ustedes están en La Paz?*
> How long have you (*pl.*) been in La Paz?

> *Hace dos días que estamos en La Paz.*
> We've been in La Paz for two days.

# Exercises

I.  Fill in the blanks with the correct forms of *servir* and *pedir:*

1. Ellos (servir) _____ la comida a las dos.

2. Francisco (pedir) _____ direcciones a la catedral.

3. ¿Va a (pedir) _____ cerveza?

4. ¿A qué hora (servir) _____ nosotros la cena?

5. Yo siempre (pedir) _____ pollo en el restaurante del hotel. Es muy bueno.

6. Nosotros (pedir) _____ información del recepcionista.

II. Fill in the blank with the appropriate prepositional phrase in Spanish:

1. Francisco va (with him) _____ al palacio.

2. Ella quiere ir (with me) _____ a Bolivia.

3. Las llaves son (for her) _____.

4. El equipo de fútbol va (with them) _____.

5. El tiene un libro de guía (for us) _____.

6. ¿Quiere ir a la catedral (with me) _____?

III. Change the following from the affirmative to the negative as in the following example:

*Javier necesita algo.*
Javier needs something.

*Javier no necesita nada.*
Javier doesn't need anything.

1. Siempre comen en el Restaurante Blanco.

2. Compran algunos vinos chilenos.

3. Hay alguien en su habitación.

4. Viajan o a Bolivia o a Colombia.

5. ¿Necesitan ustedes algo más?

IV. Replace the direct object noun with the direct object pronoun in the following sentences. Example:

Quiero ver el juego mañana.
Quiero verlo mañana *or* Lo quiero ver mañana.

1. Veo la catedral.

2. Pedimos direcciones.

3. El tiene el libro de guía.

4. Ella no juega al fútbol.

5. Nosotros tomamos la cena en el hotel.

6. Quiero ver los altares.

V.  Fill in the blanks with the correct forms of *decir, dar* and *hacer:*

1. (Hacer) _____ buen tiempo hoy.

2. El (decir) _____ que el palacio queda lejos.

3. Voy a (dar) _____ el regalo a mi hermana.

4. (Hacer) _____ una semana que estamos en el hotel.

5. Yo (hacer) _____ mucho ejercicio.

6. Francisco (decir) _____ que va a tomar un taxi.

7. Nosotras siempre (dar) _____ dinero a nuestra abuela.

## Word Study

There are two words in Spanish that mean "little," *poco* and *pequeño*, but they are not interchangeable. *Poco* means "little (in quantity)" and *pequeño* means "little (in size)."

Examples:

*Normalmente los estudiantes tienen poco dinero.*
Normally students have little money.

*La bebé, Ceci, es muy pequeña.*
Baby Ceci is very little.

## A Few Facts About Bolivia

City buses in Bolivia are called *colectivos* while intercity buses are known as *flotas*.

The native dress in Bolivia is fascinating. Knowledgeable people can identify what part of the country people come from just by their attire.

Mestizos—a mixture of Spanish American and American Indian—who emigrate to urban areas but still wear their ethnic dress are known as *cholos* (*m.*) or *cholas* (*f.*) The cholas are particularly picturesque. They wear petticoats and full skirts and wrap themselves in shawls in which they carry their babies or anything else they need to transport. The cholas from the region of La Paz are easily identifiable by their distinctive hats of the bowler type.

Bolivian cuisine is both distinctive and tasty. Highly recommended is the *empanada salteña*. It's a kind of stew of meat and chicken pieces, potato, raisins, olives and pepper sauce . . . not to be missed if you visit this country. If you have a beverage with your meal, you might want to ask for a straw. In Bolivia you'll need to ask for a *bombilla*. The word for straw varies enormously from one Spanish-speaking country to another. For example, a straw in Chile and Uruguay is a *pojita*; in Mexico, a *popote*; in Cuba, a *sorbente*; in Ecuador, a *sorbete*, and these are only a few examples.

Though Spanish is an official language of Bolivia the language of the Aymará Indians is also widely spoken. At their festivals, the Aymará Indians imbibe a highly potent drink called *chicha*.

You will be unlikely to find it in any La Paz bar or cocktail lounge. This is just as well, as drinking any potent alcoholic drink at that altitude could lead to a serious *resaca*, the word the Bolivians use for "hangover."

---

*Fútbol* in the Spanish-speaking world almost always means "soccer." Argentina however is an exception. There they use the word *balompié*. American-style "football" is closely followed by Latin Americans and is very popular with them, but they call it *fútbol americano* to differentiate between this sport and soccer.

LESSON

6

## Ir de Compras

### Diálogo

*Roberto y Laura son estudiantes universitarios argentinos y buenos amigos. Estudian arqueología y acaban de hacer un viaje a ver las ruinas incas de Machu Picchu en el Perú. Ahora están de regreso en Qosqo y están aprovechando el último día de su viaje para comprar regalos y recuerdos.*

**Roberto:** Ese viaje a Machu Picchu era el viaje más emocionante de mi vida.

**Laura:** Sí, era una experiencia maravillosa, ¿verdad?

**Roberto:** Es un viaje largo y difícil, pero vale la pena.

**Laura:** Imagínate (*fam.*) tal ciudad construida tan alta en las montañas.

**Roberto:** Bueno, aquí estamos en el mercado de artesanía. Vamos a ver lo que venden.

**Laura:** Ay, mira (*fam.*), esta tienda vende suéteres de alpaca. A mi mamá le gustan los suéteres bonitos. (al vendedor) ¿Cuánto vale este suéter azul?

**Vendedor:** Cuesta solamente 30 soles.

**Laura:** Es un poco caro para mí. ¿Puede bajar el precio un poco?

# Going Shopping

## Dialogue

*Roberto and Laura are Argentine university students and good friends. They are studying archaeology and have just made a trip to Peru to see the Incan ruins of Machu Picchu. They're now back in Qosqo and using the last day of their trip to shop for gifts and souvenirs.*

**Roberto:** That trip to Machu Picchu was the most exciting trip of my life.

**Laura:** It was a marvelous experience, wasn't it?

**Roberto:** It's a long and difficult trip but it's worth it.

**Laura:** Imagine such a city built so high in the mountains.

**Roberto:** Well, here we are in the crafts market. Let's see what they sell.

**Laura:** Oh, look, this shop sells alpaca wool sweaters. My mother likes pretty sweaters. (to the vendor) How much is this blue sweater?

**Vendedor:** It's only 30 soles.

**Laura:** It's a little too expensive. Could you lower the price a little?

**Vendedor:** Para usted, señorita, se lo doy en 25.

**Laura:** ¿Lo tiene usted en un tamaño más grande? Mi madre lleva un tamaño grande.

**Vendedor:** Creo que sí. Sí, aquí hay uno en un tamaño más grande.

**Laura:** Lo tomo.

**Roberto:** Ahora necesito un regalo para mi hermana. Allí hay una tienda que vende mantas de lana. A ella le gustan mantas bonitas para llevar por la noche.

**Laura:** Estas mantas vienen en colores tan bonitos. Allá hay una que es rosada, azul y gris que está preciosa.

**Roberto:** El color favorito de mi hermana es azul y aquí hay una que es de azul oscuro, azul claro con algo de amarillo. Tiene precio fijo y es moderado. (al vendedor) Voy a tomar esta manta, por favor.

**Laura:** Ay, mira (*fam.*), Roberto. Aquella tienda vende joyería de plata y de oro. Se dice que los precios de plata y oro en el Perú son bajos, especialmente la plata.

*En la joyería:*

**Laura:** ¡Qué joyería más hermosa! A mí me encanta la joyería.

**Roberto:** Pero para mí es algo cara.

**Shopkeeper:** For you, Miss, I'll give it to you for 25 soles.

**Laura:** Do you have it in a larger size? My mother wears a large size.

**Shopkeeper:** I think so. Yes, here's one in a larger size.

**Laura:** I'll take it.

**Roberto:** Now I need a gift for my sister. There's a shop over there that sells woolen shawls. She likes pretty shawls to wear in the evening.

**Laura:** These shawls are in such pretty colors. Over there is one in pink, blue and gray that's lovely.

**Roberto:** My sister's favorite color is blue and here's one in dark blue and light blue with a little yellow. It's a fixed price and it's reasonable. (to the shopkeeper) I'll take this shawl, please.

**Laura:** Oh, look, Roberto. That shop sells silver and gold jewelry. I understand that prices of silver and gold in Peru are low, especially the silver.

*In the jewelry store:*

**Laura:** What beautiful jewelry! I love jewelry.

**Roberto:** But I think it's rather expensive.

**Laura:** ¡Ay, me encantan estos aros de oro! Los voy a comprar.

**Roberto:** Vas (*fam.*) a gastar casi todo el resto de tu (*fam.*) dinero si lo haces (*fam.*).

**Laura:** Bueno, al menos tenemos nuestros boletos de avión de regreso.

**Roberto:** Gracias a Dios. No tengo ganas ningunas de caminar hasta la Argentina.

**Laura:** Oh, I just love these gold earrings! I'm going to buy them.

**Roberto:** You're going to spend almost all the rest of your money if you do.

**Laura:** Well, at least we have our return airline tickets.

**Roberto:** Thank heavens. I don't have any desire whatsoever to walk back to Argentina.

## Vocabulary

| | |
|---|---|
| acaban de | they have just |
| al menos | at least |
| amarillo | yellow |
| amigos | friends |
| aprovechando | taking advantage of |
| aquella | that (over there) |
| aquí | here |
| argentinos | Argentines |
| aros | earrings (*Arg.*) |
| arqueología | archaeology |
| azul | blue |
| bajar | to lower |
| bajos | low |
| boletos de avión de regreso | return airline tickets |
| bonitos | pretty |
| bueno | well |
| caminar | to walk |
| caro | expensive |
| casi | almost |
| ciudad | city |
| claro | light |
| color | color |
| comprendo | I understand |
| construida | built |
| cuesta | it costs |
| difícil | difficult |
| dinero | money |
| emocionante | exciting |
| ese | that |
| esta | this |

| | |
|---|---|
| estudian | they study |
| estudiantes | students |
| experiencia | experience |
| favorito | favorite |
| gris | gray |
| hacer un viaje | to make a trip |
| hasta | as far as |
| hermana | sister |
| hermosa | beautiful |
| imagínate | imagine (*fam.*) |
| ir de compras | to go shopping |
| joyería | jewelry store |
| le gustan mantas | she likes shawls |
| lo que | what |
| lo tomo | I'll take it |
| Machu Picchu | Quechua name meaning "ancient mountain top" |
| mantas | shawls |
| maravillosa | marvelous |
| me encanta | I [just] love |
| mercado de artesanía | crafts market |
| mira | look |
| moderado | moderate |
| montañas | mountains |
| necesito | I need |
| no tengo ganas de | I don't feel like |
| oro | gold |
| oscuro | dark |
| para llevar | to wear |
| para mí | to (for) me |
| plata | silver |

| | |
|---|---|
| precio fijo | set price |
| preciosa | lovely |
| ¿puede? | can you? |
| Qosqo | (recently changed spelling of the city of Cusco) |
| recuerdos | souvenirs |
| regalos | gifts |
| resto | rest |
| rosada | pink |
| se dice | they say |
| se lo doy en | I'll give it to you for |
| seguramente | surely |
| si | if |
| solamente | only |
| soles | currency of Perú (*sing.* sol) |
| suéteres | sweaters |
| tal | such a |
| tamaño | size |
| tienda | store |
| todo | all |
| último | last |
| universitarios | university |
| ver | to see |
| ¿verdad? | right? |
| vida | life |
| viaje | trip |

## *Expressions*

| | |
|---|---|
| Creo que sí. | I think so. |
| ¿Cuánto vale? | How much is it worth? |
| Gracias a Dios. | Thank heavens. |
| Vale la pena. | It's worth the effort. |

# Grammar

## *Demonstrative Adjectives*

Demonstrative adjectives in Spanish are the forms of adjectives that point out persons and objects. They're equivalent to the English "this," "that," "these" and "those." In Spanish, the demonstrative adjectives must agree in gender and number with the nouns they modify just as any other adjective. Their forms are as follows:

|          | Masculine | Feminine |                       |
|----------|-----------|----------|-----------------------|
| *Singular:* |        |          |                       |
|          | este      | esta     | this                  |
|          | ese       | esa      | that                  |
|          | aquel     | aquella  | that (at a distance)  |
| *Plural:* |          |          |                       |
|          | estos     | estas    | these                 |
|          | esos      | esas     | those                 |
|          | aquellos  | aquellas | those (at a distance) |

## *Verbs Having Irregular Forms in the First Person Present Tense*

It is often easier to learn irregular verbs in groups that follow the same pattern. For example, certain Spanish verbs have an irregular form in the first person singular of the present tense. Among the more common verbs that follow this pattern are:

| Verb | yo *form* |
|------|-----------|
| hacer (to do, to make) | hago |
| poner (to put, to place) | pongo |
| salir (to go out) | salgo |
| traer (to bring) | traigo |
| ver (to see) | veo |
| saber (to know, to know how) | sé |
| conocer (to know, to be acquainted with) | conozco |

The other present tense forms of the above verbs are conjugated regularly.

## Saber *vs.* Conocer

Both *saber* and *conocer* mean "to know." However, *conocer* means "to know" or "to be acquainted with" a person or place. *Saber* means to know a fact. When followed by an infinitive *saber* means "to know how to do" something. Examples:

| | |
|---|---|
| Yo sé que Lima está en el Perú. | I know (as fact) that Lima is in Peru. |
| Yo conozco a Juan muy bien. | I know Juan (as a person) very well. |
| Yo sé llegar a la catedral de aquí. | I know how to get to the cathedral from here. |

## Indirect Object Pronouns

In Lesson 5, you learned the forms of the direct object pronouns that enable you to say "She bought them," instead of "She bought the earrings." In Spanish, as in English, a sentence can have both a direct and an indirect object. They can be expressed as nouns as in "We gave the book to friends," or as pronouns, "We gave it to them." In the latter sentence "it" is the direct object pronoun and "to them" is the indirect object pronoun.

Basically, an indirect object, whether noun or pronoun, tells us to whom or for whom an action is done. Therefore, in Spanish, the indirect object pronoun includes the meaning of "to" or "for." The forms of the indirect object pronouns are as follows:

| Singular | | Plural | |
|---|---|---|---|
| me | (to, for) me | nos | (to, for) us |
| le | (to, for) him | les | (to, for) you (*pl.*) |
| | (to, for) her | | (to, for) them |
| | (to, for) you (*for.*) | | |

## Position of Object Pronouns

Normally the object pronouns go before the conjugated form of the verb, the indirect before the direct. Example: "Pedro is giving it (the book) to us," *Pedro nos lo da.* However, when object pronouns are the objects of an infinitive or a present participle they may either go before the entire verb phrase or be attached to the infinitive or present participle. "Pedro wants to give it to us," could either be *Pedro quiere dárnoslo* or *Pedro nos lo quiere dar.* "Pedro is giving it to us right now," could either be *Pedro está dándonoslo ahora mismo* or *Pedro nos lo está dando ahora mismo.* Note that when the extra syllables were added to the infinitive or to the present participle an accent was added. This is necessary to preserve the original stress.

If the direct and the indirect object pronoun forms both begin with an *l,* the indirect object form becomes *se.* Examples:

Se lo doy.              I give it (the passport) to him.

Se la compramos.       We are buying it (the blouse) for her.

A prepositional phrase can also be used with an indirect object pronoun in the same sentence for purposes of clarification or emphasis. As *le* and *les* have several meanings it may be necessary to add the prepositional phrases *a él, a ella, a usted, a ellos, a ellas* or *a ustedes.* Example:

> *Esteban le reclama el equipaje.*
> Esteban is claiming the luggage for (him, her, you).
>
> *Esteban le reclama el equipaje a ella.*
> Esteban is claiming the luggage for her.

If the indirect object of a sentence is a noun, the indirect object pronoun must also be used. This may seem redundant, but it is required. Examples:

*Le doy el pasaporte al oficial.*
I give the passport to the official.

*El hombre le vende una manta a Laura.*
The man sells a shawl to Laura.

## Gustar *and* Encantar

The Spanish verb *gustar* is used to express the idea of "to like." Literally, however, it means "to please." Therefore, to say "I like . . ." you need to change the word order so that you are, in fact, saying "_____ is pleasing to me." So to translate "I like Chilean wine" you would say "Chilean wine is pleasing to me," *Me gusta el vino chileno.* If the subject is plural as in, for example, "I like Chilean wines," you say, "Chilean wines are pleasing to me," *Me gustan los vinos chilenos.* Note the word order. The structure begins with an indirect object pronoun, is followed by the correct form of the verb *gustar* and, finally, by the subject of the sentence.

Another Spanish verb that works in the same way is *encantar.* This verb is used to express the idea "to [just] love." Literally it means "to enchant." So if you want to say "She just loves archaeology," you say archaeology enchants her, *Le encanta la arqueología.* When the subject is plural as in "Flowers enchant us," it will be expressed as *Nos encantan las flores* and will be equivalent to the English "We [just] love flowers."

## The Colors

As in English, the names of the colors are both nouns and adjectives. They are as follows:

| | |
|---|---|
| rojo | red |
| morado | purple |
| lila | lavender |
| rosado | pink |
| azul | blue |
| verde | green |
| color naranja | orange |
| moreno, pardo | brown |
| beige (*Arg.*) | |
| café (*Mex.*) | |
| marrón (*Pe., Uru., Ven.*) | |
| gris | gray |
| negro | black |
| blanco | white |

Related vocabulary:

| | |
|---|---|
| claro | light |
| pálido | pale |
| oscuro | dark |

Examples:

*Le gusta la blusa verde pálida.*
She likes the pale green blouse.

*Es un carro azul oscuro.*
It's a dark blue car.

Useful phrases regarding colors:

| | |
|---|---|
| ¿De qué color es? | What color is it? |
| ¿Cuál es su color favorito? | What's your favorite color? |
| Mi color favorito es . . . | My favorite color is . . . |

## Exercises

I. Change the following demonstrative adjectives to the correct form according to the gender and number of the noun cues:

1. esta maleta - _____ maletas

2. ese hotel - _____ hoteles

3. aquella cerveza - _____ cervezas

4. este libro - _____ libros

5. aquella cama - _____ camas

6. ese hombre - _____ hombres

II. Answer the following questions in Spanish:

1. ¿Dónde pone usted la maleta?

2. ¿Trae el libro de guía con usted?

3. ¿Sabe usted la fecha de hoy?

4. ¿Sale usted para la Argentina hoy?

5. ¿Ve usted la maleta allí?

III. Fill in the blanks with the correct forms of *saber* and *conocer:*

1. ¿Ustedes (conocer) _____ a María?

2. Ella (saber) _____ donde vive mi abuelo.

3. Yo no (saber) _____ hablar espanol bien.

4. ¿Usted (saber) _____ qué hora es?

5. Nosotros (conocer) _____ a Pedro.

6. Yo (conocer) _____ La Paz.

IV. Complete the following sentences using the correct form of the indirect object:

1. Nosotros (to you, *sing.*) _____ damos un regalo.

2. Roberto (to them) _____ dice la verdad.

3. Ella (to us) _____ da el menú.

4. Pepe (to me) _____ vende su boleto.

5. Esta señora (to you, *pl.*) _____ va a dar unos regalos.

V. Change the nouns in the following sentences to the direct and indirect object pronoun forms:

1. Doy el regalo a María.

_____

2. Traigo el menú a Pablo.

_____

3. Siempre digo la verdad a mi abuela.

_____

4. Estoy dando el equipaje al botones.

_____

5. Nosotros vamos a dar el helado a la niña.

_____

VI.   Express the following in Spanish:

    1. I like the hotel.

    2. We [just] love the book.

    3. She [just] loves this country.

    4. Does Ana like this store?

    5. I [just] love chicken.

    6. Do you like to walk?

VII.  Express the following in Spanish:

    1. the white wine

    2. that green suitcase

    3. the yellow cab

    4. this pink flower

    5. the green sweater

VIII. Respond to the following questions in Spanish:

    1. ¿Cuál es su color favorito?

    2. ¿Cuál es el color de su maleta?

    3. ¿De qué color es su suéter?

# Word Study

Most words that have double letters in English will have a single letter in Spanish. Examples:

| | |
|---|---|
| professor | *profesor* |
| possible | *posible* |
| dollar | *dólar* |
| baseball | *béisbol* |

Where the English word contains a "ph" the Spanish word will have an "f." Examples:

| | |
|---|---|
| photo | *foto* |
| phrase | *frase* |
| telephone | *teléfono* |
| pharmacy | *farmacia* |

## A Few Facts About Peru

In Peru, both city and intercity buses are called *omnibuses.* Though in many parts of Latin America an elevator is called an *elevador,* in Peru and neighboring countries the word *ascensor* is used, the word that's used in Spain.

An interesting detail about Peruvian language usage is that the word *primo,* which means "cousin" in standard Spanish, is used there as a term of address for absolutely everyone; friend, pal, buddy, neighbor, colleague, etc.

A popular dish in Peru is *lomo saltado,* stir-fried sirloin with onions and tomatoes. It's usually served with rice or French fries. Many Peruvians accompany such a meal with a judicious tot of *chicha,* an alcoholic drink made of fermented corn, peanuts or manioc. It's popular in the whole Andean region.

One particularly colorful usage of the Peruvians is the word for "hangover." They call it *la perseguidora,* or the "pursuer." And when one suffers it after imbibing a bit too much *chicha,* one does feel like the miserable thing is in pursuit.

LESSON

7

## Una Emergencia Médica

### Diálogo

Ana y Carmen son miembros de una compañía española de flamenco que está en Buenos Aires, Argentina, para empezar una gira de la región de la Plata—la Argentina, Uruguay y Paraguay. Mientras tanto, salen para ver los sitios de interés por la tarde antes de su primera función. Ana tropieza con la acera y se lastima. Ellas toman taxi a un consultorio médico. En la sala de espera:

**Ana:** ¡Ay, cómo me duele el tobillo!

**Carmen:** Vamos a ver lo que dice el médico.

**Enfermera:** El médico le puede ver ahora. Vengan ustedes por aquí.

**Médico:** Buenas tardes. Soy el doctor Sánchez. ¿En qué puedo servirle?

**Ana:** Tropecé con la acera y me caí.

**Médico:** Siéntese usted y quítese el zapato y la media. ¿Exactamente dónde está el dolor?

**Ana:** Aquí.

**Médico:** ¿Es agudo o no el dolor?

**Ana:** Es agudo, muy agudo.

# A Medical Emergency

## Dialogue

*Ana and Carmen are members of a Spanish flamenco troupe in Buenos Aires, Argentina, about to begin a tour of the La Plata region—Argentina, Uruguay and Paraguay. Meanwhile, they go out sight-seeing on the afternoon before their first performance. Ana trips on the sidewalk and hurts herself. They take a cab to a nearby doctor's office. In the waiting room:*

**Ana:** Oh, how my ankle hurts.

**Carmen:** Let's see what the doctor says.

**Nurse:** The doctor will see you now. Come this way.

**Doctor:** Good afternoon. I'm Doctor Sánchez. How can I help you?

**Ana:** I tripped on the sidewalk and fell.

**Doctor:** Sit down and take off your shoe and stocking, please. Where is the pain exactly?

**Ana:** Right here.

**Doctor:** Is the pain sharp or not?

**Ana:** It's sharp, very sharp.

**Médico:** ¿Duele cuando lo mueve?

**Ana:** Sí.

**Médico:** ¿Puede caminar algo?

**Ana:** Sí, pero me duele mucho.

*El médico examina el tobillo:*

**Médico:** Está bastante hinchado. Usted ha sufrido una torcedura. No debe caminar durante varios días. También debe ponerse hielo y elevar la pierna. Voy a darle una receta para un medicamento anti-inflamatorio. Hay una farmacia en la esquina de esta cuadra.

**Ana:** Pero doctor, soy bailadora y estoy en gira como miembro de una compañía de baile.

**Médico:** Lo siento, señorita, pero no va a estar bailando durante unos días.

**Carmen:** Ana, yo te (*fam.*) conozco. No estás (*fam.*) preocupada por perder unas funciones. Es que querías (*fam.*) instrucción en el tango con ese instructor argentino tan guapo.

**Doctor:** Does it hurt when you move it?

**Ana:** Yes, it does.

**Doctor:** Can you walk on it at all?

**Ana:** Yes, but it hurts a lot.

*The doctor examines the ankle:*

**Doctor:** It's pretty swollen. You have suffered a sprain. You shouldn't walk on it for several days. Also you should put ice on it and elevate your leg. I'm giving you a prescription for an anti-inflammatory medication. There's a pharmacy at the end of this block.

**Ana:** But doctor, I'm a dancer and I'm on tour as a member of a dance group.

**Doctor:** I'm sorry, miss. You won't be dancing the next couple of days.

**Carmen:** Ana, I know you. You're not worried about missing a few performances. It's that you wanted instruction in tango with that handsome Argentine instructor.

## Vocabulary

| | |
|---|---|
| acera | sidewalk |
| agudo | sharp |
| al final | at the end |
| algo | a bit |
| antes de | before |
| anti-inflamatorio | anti-inflammatory |
| aquí | here |
| bailadora | dancer |
| bastante | rather |
| caminar | to walk |
| ¿cómo? | how? |
| compañía | troupe |
| consultorio médico | doctor's office |
| cuadra | block |
| debe | he/she/you should |
| dolor | pain |
| durante | during |
| elevar | to elevate |
| empezar | to begin |
| en | in |
| española | Spanish |
| exactamente | exactly |
| examina | he examines |
| farmacia | pharmacy |
| función | performance |
| gira | tour |
| ha sufrido | you have suffered |
| hielo | ice |
| hinchado | swollen |
| instrucción | instruction |
| lo mueve | you move it |

| | |
|---|---|
| me caí | I fell |
| me duele | it hurts me |
| media | stocking |
| medicamento | medication |
| médico | doctor; medical |
| miembros | members |
| mientras que | while |
| para | in order to |
| parte | part |
| pierna | leg |
| ponerse | to put on |
| por perder | about missing |
| preocupada | worried |
| quítese | take off |
| receta | prescription |
| región | region |
| sala de espera | waiting room |
| se lastima | hurts herself |
| siéntese | sit (yourself) down |
| sobre | on |
| tobillo | ankle |
| torcedura | sprain |
| tropecé | I tripped on |
| tropieza | trips over |
| varios | several |
| vengan | come |
| zapato | shoe |

## Expressions

| | |
|---|---|
| ¿En qué puedo servirle? | How can I help you? |
| Lo siento. | I'm sorry. |

# Grammar

## Demonstrative Pronouns

Demonstrative pronouns are exactly the same as the demonstrative adjectives except that they bear an accent over the stressed syllable, allowing one to differentiate in writing which is the adjective and which is the pronoun. The pronouns are as follows:

| **Masculine** | | **Feminine** | | |
|---|---|---|---|---|
| *Sing.* | *Plural* | *Sing.* | *Plural* | |
| éste | éstos | ésta | éstas | this (one), these |
| ése | ésos | ésa | ésas | that (one), those |
| aquél | aquéllos | aquélla | aquéllas | that (one), those (in the distance) |

Examples:

*¿Quiere comprar esta manta o ésa?*
Do you want to buy this shawl or that one? (that one near you)

*No quiero comprar ésta. Quiero comprar aquélla.*
I don't want to buy this one (near the person answering the question). I want that one (that one distant from both the person asking the question and the person answering).

## Reflexive Verbs

In many sentences the subject of the verb acts on other persons or things. Example:

> *Ella baña al bebé.*
> She bathes the baby.

However, the subject of the verb often acts on itself as well. The verb forms used in this case are called reflexive verbs. Example:

> *Ella se baña.*
> She bathes herself. (She takes a bath.)

Reflexive verbs use the reflexive pronouns to direct the action back to the subject. They are as follows:

| Subject pronouns | Reflexive pronouns | |
|---|---|---|
| yo | me | myself, to/for myself |
| él | se | himself, to/for himself |
| ella | se | herself, to/for herself |
| usted | se | yourself (*for.*), to/for yourself |
| nosotros/-as | nos | ourselves, to/for ourselves |
| ellos/ellas | se | themselves, to/for themselves |
| ustedes | se | yourselves, to/for yourselves |

Except for the third person singular and plural *se* forms, the reflexive pronouns have the same forms as the direct and indirect object pronouns.

As with the direct and indirect object pronouns, the reflexive pronouns are normally placed before the conjugated form of the verb. When they are the objects of an infinitive or present participle, however, they may either go before the entire verb phrase or after and be attached. Examples:

Ella se va a bañar.   *or*  Ella va a bañarse.
She's going to take a bath.

Ella se está bañando.   *or*  Ella está bañándose.
She's taking a bath.

Present tense of *bañarse*

| | |
|---|---|
| yo me baño | I bathe (myself) |
| él se baña | he bathes (himself) |
| ella se baña | she bathes (herself) |
| usted se baña | you (*for.*) bathe (yourself) |
| nosotros/-as nos bañamos | we bathe (ourselves) |
| ellos se bañan | they (*m.*) bathe (themselves) |
| ellas se bañan | they (*f.*) bathe (themselves) |
| ustedes se bañan | you (*pl.*) bathe (yourselves) |

Other common reflexive verbs include:

| | |
|---|---|
| levantar(se) | to get up |
| lavar(se) | to wash up |
| vestir(se) (e to i) | to get dressed |
| quitar(se) | to take off |
| acostar(se) (o to ue) | to go to bed |
| poner(se) | to put on |
| lastimar(se) | to get hurt |

In vocabulary lists, reflexive verbs are identified by the *se* form, attached to the infinitive as above.

The Spanish reflexive forms of the verb are often equivalent to what, in English, are called two-word verbs, where a preposition is added to the verb: "take off," "put on," "wake up," "sit down," etc.

## Formal Commands

Commands are the forms of the verb used to tell someone to do something, as in "Buy the gift," and "Take the luggage up to the room." In Spanish, the formal usted/ustedes commands are formed by dropping the *o* of the *yo* form of the present tense and adding *e* or *en* for *-ar* verbs and *a* or *an* for *-er* and *-ir* verbs. Examples:

|            | Infinitive | Usted  | Ustedes  |
|------------|-----------|--------|----------|
| -ar verbs  | comprar   | compre | compren  |
| -er verbs  | comer     | coma   | coman    |
| -ir verbs  | decidir   | decida | decidan  |

There are, predictably, a number of formal commands that are irregular. They include the following:

|       | Usted  | Ustedes |
|-------|--------|---------|
| ir    | vaya   | vayan   |
| ser   | sea    | sean    |
| dar   | dé     | den     |
| poner | ponga  | pongan  |
| salir | salga  | salgan  |
| tener | tenga  | tengan  |
| estar | esté   | estén   |
| traer | traiga | traigan |
| saber | sepa   | sepan   |

To soften a command, put the *usted* form after the command and follow it with "please," *por favor.* If you are giving a series of commands, you need only use *usted* with the first one.

> *Traiga usted la cuenta, por favor.*
> Bring the bill, please.

> *Suba* (usted) *el equipaje, por favor.*
> Take the luggage up, please.

To make a command negative, simply put *no* before the command form. Examples:

> *No compre esa blusa. Es muy cara.*
> Don't buy that blouse. It's very expensive.

> *No ponga la maleta en la habitación.*
> Don't put the suitcase in the room.

As to the position of object pronouns with commands, they are placed after and attached to affirmative commands, that is, commands telling someone to do something.

| | |
|---|---|
| Cómprela. | Buy it (the blouse). |
| Hágalo ahora. | Do it now. |

In negative commands, that is, commands telling someone not to do something, object pronouns are always placed before the verb.

| | |
|---|---|
| No la compre. | Don't buy it (the blouse). |
| No lo haga. | Don't do it. |

Note: The rules for position are the same for double object pronouns. Just remember that the indirect object pronoun always goes before the direct object pronoun and that if both pronouns begin with *l*, the indirect object pronoun is changed to *se*.

## The Idiom Acabar de + Infinitive

The Spanish infinitive *acabar* means "to finish." But when used with the preposition *de* plus an infinitive it conveys the meaning of "to have just." Examples:

> *Acabo de comer un postre.*
> I have just eaten a dessert.

> *Acabamos de caminar al hotel.*
> We have just walked to the hotel.

## Exercises

I.  Answer the following questions, responding with the demonstrative pronouns:

1. ¿Quiere usted estos libros o ésos?

2. ¿Quiere usted este vino o éste?

3. ¿Quiere usted esa mesa o aquélla?

4. ¿Quiere este postre o ése?

5. ¿Quiere estos libros o aquéllos?

II.  Rewrite the following sentences according to the cues in parentheses. Example:

> Nosotros nos sentamos. (Él)
> Él se sienta.

1. Ella se baña todas las mañanas. (Yo)

2. Ellos se quitan los zapatos. (Ella)

3. Yo me acuesto a las once. (Juan)

4. Ella se lava las manos. (Yo)

5. Nosotras nos ponemos los suéteres. (Ellos)

III.  Give the formal <u>singular</u> command forms of the following and soften with *por favor.* Example:

> abrir el libro
> Abra (usted) el libro, por favor.

1. traer la cuenta

2. hablar más despacio

3. ir a migración

4. salir del carro

5. subir el equipaje

6. hacer la reservación

IV. Give the formal <u>plural</u> command forms of the above and soften with *por favor.* Example:

   abrir el libro    Abran (ustedes) el libro, por favor.

V. Express the following in Spanish:

   1. We have just claimed our luggage.

   2. She has just bought the earrings.

   3. I have just put the papers on the table.

   4. They have just brought the suitcase to their room.

   5. Ana has just gone to the doctor's office.

## Word Study

There are two verbs in Spanish that mean "to play," but they are not interchangeable. *Jugar* (*ue*) means "to play (a game)" whereas *tocar* means "to play (a musical instrument)."

Examples:

> *Manuel juega al fútbol.*
> Manuel plays soccer.

> *Su hermana toca muy bien la guitarra.*
> His sister plays the guitar very well.

## A Few Facts About The River Plate Region

The part of South America known as the *La Plata,* or "River Plate" region strictly speaking includes only Argentina and Uruguay. However, because of its geographic proximity Paraguay will also be mentioned in this lesson.

This region is linguistically interesting for a variety of reasons. To begin with, its pronunciation is quite distinctive. People who are savvy about the Spanish language will recognize an Argentine accent immediately. It's principal characteristic is the pronunciation of *y* and *ll.* In most parts of the Spanish-speaking world these letters are pronounced like the "y" in the English word "canyon." These same letters in Argentina, as well as in nearby areas of the "Cone of South America," are pronounced "shsss," rather like the sound a librarian makes when you're making too much noise in the library.

Another interesting detail about the language of this region is the use of the word *vos* as the familiar singular form of the subject pronoun "you." This shouldn't present a problem for the casual traveler because it is ill advised that such a person use the familiar form of "you" under any circumstances. It is still useful to know that this word is the familiar form used in this region.

The region of Argentina, Uruguay and to a lesser extent Paraguay has a large European population, principally Spanish, Italian and German. This has had an enormous influence on the language spoken there. In Argentina, the influence is principally Italian. For example, the famous Argentine who became a leader of the Cuban Revolution, Ernesto "Che" Guevara, owed his nickname "Che" to the Italian word for "buddy," or "pal," or just "Hey there."

Still another element in the linguistic complexity of this region is the existence of a type of Argentine slang known as *Lunfardo*. It is something of a mix of *Gallego* (the Spanish spoken in the Spanish province of Galicia), Italian and French. This slang has greatly influenced the Spanish of Argentina. For example, lawyers are known as *abogados* in most of the Spanish-speaking world. In Argentina, the word often used is simply *bogas*, the word for "lawyers" in Lunfardo. What is a meal in most Spanish-speaking countries, a *comida*, is called a *morfi* in Lunfardo.

To a certain extent, this slang is known in neighboring countries. In Paraguay, however, the principal influence is from the indigenous language, *Guaraní*. This language is, in fact, an official language as is Spanish.

Vegetarians will not be altogether happy in this region. Meat is the favored food.

## Vocabulary For Emergencies

One would hope never to have to face an emergency situation in a foreign country. However, there are no guarantees that it won't happen. So some words and phrases should be learned well and early in one's language study. They include:

| | |
|---|---|
| ¡Socorro! ¡Auxilio! | Help! |
| ¡Es una emergencia! | It's an emergency! |
| ¡Llame a un médico (doctor)! | Call a doctor! |
| ¡Llame una ambulancia! | Call an ambulance! |
| Estoy enfermo/a. | I'm sick. (*m./f.*) |
| ¡Ladrón! | Thief! |
| ¡Policia! | Police! |
| ¡Me han robado! | I've been robbed! |
| ¡Fuego! | Fire! |
| ¡Cuidado! | Watch out! |

# LESSON
## 8

# Las Comunicaciones

## Diálogo

*Un matrimonio jubilado, los señores Martínez, están en Guayaquil, Ecuador, en camino hacia las Islas Galápagos. Les encantan los animales y para ellos este viaje es el sueño de toda la vida. Su vecina, Marta, está cuidando su gato en casa mientras que están de viaje:*

**Sra. Martínez:** Yo quiero llamar a Marta antes de tomar el avión mañana para ver si está bien el gato.

**Sr. Martínez:** Está bien, pero no del hotel. Las llamadas de larga distancia valen caro en el hotel. Mejor que compremos una tarjeta telefónica. Son más baratas.

*Compran su tarjeta y buscan teléfono público. La señora Martínez mete la tarjeta y marca el número:*

**Sra. Martínez:** Suena y suena pero no contesta nadie.

**Sr. Martínez:** Puedes (*fam.*) intentar otra vez más tarde, mamá. Mientras tanto vamos a comprar tarjetas postales aquí en este quiosco y entonces podemos tomar un café y escribirlas.

*Tomando café, el matrimonio escribe varias tarjetas para enviar a su familia y a varios amigos:*

**Sr. Martínez:** (al mozo) Señor, ¿puede usted decirnos dónde queda la casa de correos?

**Mozo:** Sí, señor. Queda cerca. Hay que doblar en esta esquina y caminar como tres cuadras.

# Communications

## Dialogue

*A retired couple, Mr. and Mrs. Martínez, are in Guayaquil, Ecuador, on their way to the Galápagos Islands. They just love animals and for them this trip is the dream of a lifetime. Martha, a neighbor of theirs, is taking care of their cat back home while they're on the trip:*

**Mrs. Martínez:** I want to call the neighbor before taking the plane tomorrow to see if the cat's OK.

**Mr. Martínez:** All right, but not from the hotel. Long distance calls are so expensive from the hotel. It's better that we buy a telephone card. They're much cheaper.

*They buy the card and look for a public telephone. Ms. Martínez puts in the card and punches in the number:*

**Mrs. Martínez:** It's ringing and ringing but no one answers.

**Mr. Martínez:** You can try again later, mother. Meanwhile, let's buy postcards here in this stand and then we can have coffee and write them.

*Over coffee, the couple writes several postcards to send to family and friends:*

**Mr. Martínez:** (to the waiter) Sir, can you tell us where the post office is from here?

**Waiter:** Yes, sir. It's nearby. You have to turn right at the corner and walk about three blocks.

**Sr. Martínez:** Muchas gracias.

*Llegan a la esquina y la señora Martínez ve un cybercafé:*

**Sra. Martínez:** Mira (*fam.*), aquí puedo mandar correo electrónico a Marta. Ella está en línea. Voy a preguntarle si está bien el gato.

**Sr. Martínez:** Si tú insistes (*fam.*).

*Al fin, llegan a Correos:*

**Sr. Martínez:** (al empleado de Correos) ¿Cuánto cuestan los sellos para tarjetas postales?

**Empleado de Correos:** ¿Domésticos o internacionales?

**Sr. Martínez:** Domésticos.

*El empleado le muestra los sellos y el señor Martínez compra seis:*

**Sr. Martínez:** (al empleado) ¿Y dónde está el buzón?

**Empleado de Correos:** Allí al lado de la puerta principal.

**Sr. Martínez:** Gracias.

**Sra. Martínez:** Mira (*fam.*), tienen servicio de fax aquí. Le voy a mandar un fax a Marta por si acaso no llega bien el correo electrónico. No quiero salir de Guayaquil sin noticias del gato.

**Sr. Martínez:** (ya un poco impaciente) ¡Mamá, mejor mándale a Félix una tarjeta postal y ya!

**Mr. Martínez:** Thanks a lot.

*They arrive at the corner and Mrs. Martínez sees a cybercafé:*

**Mrs. Martínez:** Look, here I can send an e-mail to Marta. She's on the Net. I'm going to ask her whether there's any problem with the cat.

**Mr. Martínez:** If you insist.

*Finally they arrive at the post office:*

**Mr. Martínez:** (to the postal worker) How much do stamps for postcards cost?

**Postal worker:** Domestic or international?

**Mr. Martínez:** Domestic.

*The worker shows him the stamps and Mr. Martínez buys six:*

**Mr. Martínez:** And where is the mailbox?

**Postal worker:** Over there, beside the door.

**Mr. Martínez:** Thanks.

**Mrs. Martínez:** Look, they have fax service here. I'm going to send Marta a fax just in case the e-mail doesn't get there. I don't want to leave here without news of the cat.

**Mr. Martínez:** (a little impatient by now) Mother, why don't you send Felix a postcard and let it go at that!

## *Vocabulary*

| | |
|---|---|
| a la derecha | to the right |
| al lado | beside |
| allí | over there |
| animales | animals |
| antes de | before |
| aquí | here |
| avión | plane |
| baratas | cheap |
| buscan | they look for |
| buzón | mailbox |
| caminar | to walk |
| como | about |
| correo electrónico | e-mail |
| correos | post office |
| cuadras | blocks |
| cuestan | cost |
| de larga distancia | long distance |
| decirnos | tell us |
| desde | from |
| domésticos | domestic |
| empleado de correos | postal worker |
| en camino hacia | on the way to |
| entonces | then |
| enviar | to send |
| escribe | writes |
| escribirlas | to write them |
| esquina | corner |
| está cuidando | is taking care of |
| familia | family |
| gato | cat |

| | |
|---|---|
| impaciente | impatient |
| intentar | to try |
| internacionales | international |
| islas | islands |
| jubilado | retired |
| llamadas | calls |
| llamar | to call |
| mándale | send him |
| mandar | to send |
| marca | marks |
| matrimonio | married couple |
| mesero | waiter |
| mete | sticks in |
| mientras tanto | meanwhile |
| mira | look (*fam.*) |
| muestra | shows |
| otra vez | again |
| podemos | we can |
| preguntar | to ask |
| puedes | you can (*fam.*) |
| puerta principal | main door |
| queda cerca | it's nearby |
| quiosco | stand |
| sellos | stamps |
| servicio de fax | fax service |
| sin noticias | without news |
| sobre café | over coffee |
| suena y suena | it rings and rings |
| sueño | dream |
| tarjeta telefónica | phone card |
| tarjetas postales | postcards |
| teléfono público | pay phone |

| | |
|---|---|
| toda la vida | a lifetime |
| tomar | taking |
| valen caro | are expensive |
| varias | several |
| ve | she sees |
| vecina | neighbor |
| ver | to see |
| ya | by now |
| ¡y ya! | and let it go at that (literally: and that's enough) |

## Expressions

| | |
|---|---|
| Ella está en línea. | She's on-line. |
| No contesta nadie. | No one's answering. |
| Por si acaso. | Just in case. |
| Si tú insistes. | If you insist. (*fam.*) |

# Grammar

## Preterit Tense of Regular Verbs

In Spanish, there are two simple past tenses, the preterit and the imperfect. The preterit is the tense that indicates a one-time action in the past that is over and done with. The preterit would be used to convey such information as, "He went to Santiago last Monday" or "Carlos bought the gift yesterday."

The preterit of regular -ar verbs is formed by dropping the -ar and adding the endings -é, -ó, -amos and -aron, as follows:

comprar (to buy)

| | |
|---|---|
| yo compré | I bought |
| él/ella/usted compró | he/she/you (for.) bought |
| nosotros/-as compramos | we bought |
| ellos/ellas/ustedes compraron | they/you (pl.) bought |

The preterit of regular -er and -ir verbs is formed by dropping the -er or -ir and adding the endings -í, -ió, -imos and -ieron, as follows:

comer (to eat)

| | |
|---|---|
| yo comí | I ate |
| él/ella/usted comió | he/she/you (for.) ate |
| nosotros/-as comimos | we ate |
| ellos/ellas/ustedes comieron | they/you (pl.) ate |

*vivir* (to live)

| | |
|---|---|
| yo viví | I lived |
| él/ella/usted vivió | he/she/you (*for.*) lived |
| nosotros/-as vivimos | we lived |
| ellos/ellas/ustedes vivieron | they/you (*pl.*) lived |

## Preterit Tense of Some Irregular Verbs

There are a number of verbs that are irregular in the preterit tense. The following are among the most common ones:

*ser* (to be)

| | |
|---|---|
| yo fui | I was |
| él/ella/usted fue | he/she was, |
| | you (*for.*) were |
| nosotros/-as fuimos | we were |
| ellos/ellas/ustedes fueron | they/you (*pl.*) were |

The preterit tense forms of *ir* are exactly the same as the preterit of *ser*. Only context makes it clear which verb these forms represent.

*ir* (to go)

| | |
|---|---|
| yo fui | I went |
| él/ella/usted fue | he/she/you (*for.*) went |
| nosotros/-as fuimos | we went |
| ellos/ellas/ustedes fueron | they/you (*pl.*) went |

*estar* (to be)

| | |
|---|---|
| yo estuve | I was |
| él/ella/usted estuvo | he/she was, you (*for.*) were |
| nosotros/-as estuvimos | we were |
| ellos/ellas/ustedes estuvieron | they/you (*pl.*) were |

*tener* (to have)

| | |
|---|---|
| yo tuve | I had |
| él/ella/usted tuvo | he/she/you (*for.*) had |
| nosotros/-as tuvimos | we had |
| ellos/ellas/ustedes tuvieron | they/you (*pl.*) had |

*dar* (to give)

| | |
|---|---|
| yo di | I gave |
| él/ella/usted dio | he/she/you (*for.*) gave |
| nosotros/-as dimos | we gave |
| ellos/ellas/ustedes dieron | they/you (*pl.*) gave |

*poner* (to put, to place)

| | |
|---|---|
| yo puse | I put |
| él/ella/usted puso | he/she/you (*for.*) put |
| nosotros/-as pusimos | we put |
| ellos/ellas/ustedes pusieron | they/you (*pl.*) put |

*venir* (to come)

| | |
|---|---|
| yo vine | I came |
| él/ella/usted vino | he/she/you (*for.*) came |
| nosotros/-as venimos | we came |
| ellos/ellas/ustedes vinieron | they/you (*pl.*) came |

*poder* (can, to be able to)

| | |
|---|---|
| yo pude | I was able to |
| él/ella/usted pudo | he/she was able to, you (*for.*) were able to |
| nosotros/-as pudimos | we were able to |
| ellos/ellas/ustedes pudieron | they/you (*pl.*) were able to |

Note: *Poder* in the preterit means "to be able" in the sense of "to manage." Example:

*Luis pudo abrir la puerta.*
Luis managed to open the door.

*decir* (to say)

| | |
|---|---|
| yo dije | I said |
| él/ella/usted dijo | he/she/you (*for.*) said |
| nosotros/-as dijimos | we said |
| ellos/ellas/ustedes dijeron | they/you (*pl.*) said. |

## Pedir *vs.* Preguntar

Both *pedir* and *preguntar* mean "to ask." The verb *pedir* means "to ask *for*," "to request" or "to order" something.

Examples:

*Pido postre.*
I am ordering dessert.

*Pedimos la llave en la Recepción.*
We asked for the key at the reception desk.

The verb *preguntar* means "to ask" in the sense of asking a question or requesting some type of information. Here are two examples:

*Ellos preguntan dónde está la catedral.*
They ask where the cathedral is.

*Voy a preguntarle a abuela si la cena está lista.*
I'm going to ask grandma if dinner is ready.

## Sino *vs.* Pero

The Spanish words *sino* and *pero* both mean "but." *Sino* means "but" in the sense of "but rather" and is only used in negative statements:

*No es el hotel caro sino el hotel de precio moderado.*
It's not the expensive hotel but (rather) the modest-priced hotel.

*Pero* is used for "but" in all other cases:

*El hotel es de precio moderado, pero es cómodo.*
The hotel is modest in price but it's comfortable.

## Exercises

I.  Change the following sentences from the future substitute (*ir a* + infinitive) to the preterit (simple past tense) according to the word or phrase in parentheses. Example:

Yo voy a reclamar el equipaje. (ayer)
Yo reclamé el equipaje ayer.

1. Nosotros vamos a comer en el hotel. (ayer)

2. Ella va a estudiar. (esta mañana)

3. Ellos van a abrir el regalo. (el martes)

4. Voy a comprar la maleta. (anoche)

5. Mañana ellos van a viajar. (ayer)

II. Fill in the blanks with the correct irregular preterit form of the verbs in parentheses:

1. Ellas nos (dar) _____ el equipaje.

2. Mi abuela (venir) _____ ayer.

3. Nosotros (ir) _____ a un buen restaurante para comer.

4. La fiesta (ser) _____ ayer.

5. ¿(Ir) _____ ellos a Santiago de Chile?

6. Juanita le (dar) _____ un libro de guía.

7. ¿Dónde (poner) _____ Esteban la maleta?

8. Yo no (poder) _____ ir a Machu Picchu.

9. Manuel (decir) _____ la verdad.

10. ¿Dónde (estar) _____ ustedes anoche?

III. Express the following in Spanish:

1. She sold her book.

2. Alfredo wrote the postcard to his sister.

3. Did you see the doctor?

4. I went to Buenos Aires in May.

5. They received the gift.

6. We ate the delicious dessert.

7. Bernardo understood the directions.

8. My grandmother visited us in October.

9. Mr. and Mrs. Vásquez came to our house.

10. Elena told Ana where we lived.

IV. Express the following in Spanish:

1. She asks what time it is.

2. Carlos always orders Chilean wine.

3. When I don't know, I ask Joel.

4. Elena asked for the money.

5. When the students don't understand something in the lesson, they ask the professor.

V. Fill in the blanks with *sino* or *pero* as appropriate:

1. El suéter no es morado, _____ lila.

2. Pedro viaja mucho, _____ no vende mucho.

3. El hotel es pequeño, _____ cómodo.

4. No es grande la maleta, _____ pequeña.

5. No como en casa, _____ en un restaurante.

## Word Study

Many words that begin with "s" in English begin with *es* in Spanish. Examples:

| | |
|---|---|
| station | *estación* |
| special | *especial* |
| stomach | *estómago* |
| strict | *estricto* |
| style | *estilo* |

## A Few Facts About Ecuador

Nestled as it is directly to the north of Peru, Ecuador shares many linguistic characteristics with its Andean neighbors. For example, just as in Chile, a *guagua* is a baby and not a bus as it is in the Caribbean. Likewise, an elevator in Ecuador is an *ascensor* rather than an *elevador*.

Ecuador does also have its words, however, that are specific to the country. One of them is the word for "hangover," *chuchaqui*, a word clearly of Indian origin. "Hangover" is one of those words that seems to vary greatly from country to country. Another such word is "popcorn." In Ecuador, it's called *canguil*.

The Galápagos Islands, mentioned in this lesson's introductory dialogue, are often referred to in Ecuador as *las Islas Encantadas*, "the Enchanted Islands." Their name, Galápagos, is the word for the giant sea turtles that abound there. Due to its unique fauna these islands have been included on the list of the patrimony of humanity. It was here that Darwin developed his theory of the evolution of the species.

Communication from the major cities of Ecuador to the outside world is excellent. Most particularly available is public access to the Internet. What are known variously as cybercafés or Internet Cafés are springing up like mushrooms. There are streets in Quito that boast of three or four of such enterprises with more opening almost daily. Beyond offering basic Internet services, these entities also offer food service ranging from water and snacks to hot sit-down lunches. At least one even offers cocktails after 5:00 P.M.

Ecuador has just converted its currency from the *sucre* to the dollar, *el dólar.*

Some decorative separator

As long as one is in an urban area, all types of long distance communication from Latin America are excellent. Urban cities from the Río Grande to the tip of Patagonia have full phone, fax and Internet service. Regular mail, however, is exceptionally slow. The "snails" apparently always take the scenic route.

LESSON

9

# Viajando por Carro

## Diálogo

*Miguel y Carlos, jóvenes ecologistas, acaban de participar en una conferencia sobre el medio ambiente en San José, Costa Rica. Acaban de rentar un carro y están viajando por varios países en América Central:*

**Miguel:** Esto debe ser una gran aventura. Tengo ganas de ver tanta fauna y flora que podemos ver.

**Carlos:** La conferencia era maravillosa ¿verdad? Costa Rica tiene un verdadero interés en la ecología de esta región. Y los ticos son tan amables. Era un verdadero placer participar en una conferencia allí.

**Miguel:** El hombre en la agencia de carros de renta era especialmente amable. Yo estaba algo nervioso con la idea de viajar por carro por la América Central, pero todos sus consejos me hacían sentir más seguro.

**Carlos:** Su explicación de las leyes de tránsito de los varios países era muy útil.

**Miguel:** Pues el consejo de no manejar por la noche era bastante importante también.

**Carlos:** Y era bueno saber que las carreteras principales son bastante buenas.

**Miguel:** ¡Ay, mira *(fam.)*! Hay una gasolinera allí adelante. Vamos a parar y comprar gasolina.

# Travel by Car

## *Dialogue*

*Miguel and Carlos, young environmentalists, have just partici-*
*pated in a conference on the environment in San José, Costa*
*Rica. They have just rented a car and are traveling through sev-*
*eral Central American countries:*

**Miguel:** This should be a great adventure. I have a desire to see
as much of the flora and fauna as we can see.

**Carlos:** The conference was wonderful, wasn't it? Costa Rica has
a true interest in the ecology of this region. And the Ticos are so
nice. It was a real pleasure to participate in a conference there.

**Miguel:** The man in the car rental agency was especially nice.
I was a little nervous about traveling by car in Central America,
but all of his advice made me feel more secure.

**Carlos:** His explanation of the different traffic laws in the various countries was very useful.

**Miguel:** Well, the advice not to drive at night was pretty important, too.

**Carlos:** And it was good to know that the main highways are
pretty good.

**Miguel:** Oh, look! There's a gas station up ahead. Let's stop and
get gas.

**Carlos:** Pero todavía tenemos medio tanque.

**Miguel:** Recuerda (*fam.*) lo que nos dijo el agente en la agencia de renta que a veces hay mucha distancia entre las gasolineras.

**Carlos:** Verdad que sí. Entonces vamos a parar para comprar gasolina.

**Carlos:** (al gasolinero) Llénelo, por favor. Y revise el aceite.

**Miguel:** Pero todo fue revisado cuando rentamos el carro en la frontera hondureña.

**Carlos:** Verdad que sí. No debemos tener ningún problema con la batería, los frenos, las llantas . . .

**Carlos:** (al gasolinero) ¿Puede usted decirnos a cuántos kilómetros queda Tegucigalpa de aquí?

**Gasolinero:** No está lejos. Queda a eso de 35 kilómetros de aquí. Pero tengan cuidado cuando ustedes se acercan de la ciudad. Hay muchos túmulos y son bien grandes.

**Carlos:** Muchas gracias. ¿Cuánto le debemos?

*El gasolinero señala el precio en la bomba de gasolina.*

*Los ecologistas siguen hacia la ciudad:*

**Miguel:** ¡Ay, dios mío! Hay una bandada de guacamayos en aquel árbol. Vamos a parar. Agarra (*fam.*) la cámara.

**Carlos:** But we've still got over a half a tank.

**Miguel:** Remember what the rental agent told us, that sometimes there's a long way between gas stations.

**Carlos:** Right. So let's stop and get gas.

**Carlos:** (to the gas station attendant) Fill it up, please. And check the oil.

**Miguel:** But everything was checked when we rented the car at the Honduran border.

**Carlos:** True, we shouldn't have any problems with the battery, brakes, tires...

**Carlos:** (to the gas station attendant) Can you tell us how many kilometers it is to Tegucigalpa?

**Gas station attendant:** It's not far. It's about 35 kilometers. But be careful as you approach the city. There are a lot of speed bumps and they're very high.

**Carlos:** Thanks a lot. How much do we owe you?

*The gas station attendant points to the amount on the gas pump.*

*The two environmentalists head for the city:*

**Miguel:** Oh good heavens! There's a flock of macaws in that tree. Let's stop! Grab the camera.

*Los jóvenes sacan fotos y siguen por el camino:*

**Carlos:** Necesitamos llegar a Tegucigalpa antes del anochecer. Y tú sabes (*fam.*), es sábado y hay mucha fiesta los fines de semana en estas partes. Probablemente debemos quedar en la ciudad hasta el lunes.

**Miguel:** Quizás alguién nos invita a nosotros a una fiesta. No tenemos apuro.

**Carlos:** Verdad que sí. Recuerda (*fam.*) lo que nos dijo el agente de renta . . . que por aquí los fines de semana la especie más amenazada es el motorista.

*The young men take pictures and then continue on the road:*

**Carlos:** We need to get to Tegucigalpa before nightfall. And you know, it's Saturday and there's a lot of partying that goes on in these parts. We should probably stay in the city until Monday.

**Miguel:** Maybe somebody will invite us to a party. We're in no hurry.

**Carlos:** Right. Remember what the car rental agent told us . . . that over the weekends the most endangered species here is the motorist.

## Vocabulary

| | |
|---|---|
| aceite | oil |
| a eso de | approximately |
| adelante | up ahead |
| agarra | grab (*fam.*) |
| agencia | agency |
| amables | nice |
| anochecer | nightfall |
| antes de | before |
| árbol | tree |
| aventura | adventure |
| bandada | flock |
| bastante | rather |
| batería | battery |
| bien grandes | really big |
| buenas | good |
| cámara | camera |
| camino | road |
| carreteras | highways |
| carro | car |
| ciudad | city |
| conferencia | conference |
| consejos | advice |
| ecología | ecology |
| ecologistas | environmentalists |
| en estas partes | around here |
| encontrar | to find |
| entonces | then |
| entre | between |
| especie amenazada | endangered species |
| explicarnos | to explain to us |
| fauna y flora | flora and fauna |

| | |
|---|---|
| fiesta | partying; party |
| fines de semana | weekends |
| frenos | brakes |
| frontera | border |
| fue revisado | was checked |
| gasolina | gas |
| gasolinera | gas station |
| gasolinero | gas station attendant |
| gran | great |
| guacamayos | macaws |
| hombre | man |
| hondureña | Honduran |
| importante | important |
| interés | interest |
| jóvenes | young |
| kilómetros | kilometers |
| leyes de tránsito | traffic laws |
| llantas | tires |
| llénelo | fill it up |
| manejar | to drive |
| maravillosa | marvelous |
| medio ambiente | environment |
| medio tanque | half a tank |
| mira | look (*fam.*) |
| motorista | motorist |
| nervioso | nervous |
| ningún | no |
| no tenemos apuro | we're not in a hurry |
| nos dijo | he/she told us |
| países | countries |
| parar | to stop |
| participar | to participate |
| placer | pleasure |

| | |
|---|---|
| podemos | we can |
| por la noche | at night |
| por | through |
| principales | main |
| probablemente | probably |
| quedar | to stay |
| quizás | perhaps |
| recuerda | remember (*fam.*) |
| región | region |
| renta de carros | car rental |
| rentar | to rent |
| revise | check |
| sabes | you know (*fam.*) |
| sacan fotos | they take pictures |
| se acercan | you (*pl.*) approach |
| seguro | secure |
| sentir | to feel |
| siguen | continue on |
| sobre | about |
| también | too |
| todavía | still |
| túmulos | speed bumps (*C.A.*) |
| verdadero | real |
| viajando | traveling |

### Expressions

| | |
|---|---|
| ¡Dios mío! | Good heavens! |
| Tenga cuidado. | Be (*sing.*) careful. |
| Tengan cuidado. | Be (*pl.*) careful. |
| Verdad que sí. | That's true. |

# Grammar

## Formation of Regular Verbs in the Imperfect Tense

As you learned in Lesson 8, there are two simple past tenses in Spanish, the preterit and the imperfect. It was pointed out that the preterit tense reflects an action in the past that is over and done with.

The imperfect tense emphasizes the action in progress and is not concerned with when that action ended. Typically, this tense is equivalent to the English "was, were" plus the present participle, the simple past form, or the structure "used to" plus infinitive.

To form the imperfect of -ar verbs, drop the -ar and add the endings -aba, -aba, ábamos and -aban, as follows:

buscar (to look for, to seek)

| | |
|---|---|
| yo buscaba | I was looking for, looked for, used to look for |
| él/ella/usted buscaba | he/she was looking for, looked for, used to look for, you (for.) were looking for, looked for, used to look for |
| nosotros/-as buscábamos | we were looking for, looked for, used to look for |

ellos/ellas/ustedes buscaban    they/you (*pl.*) were looking for, looked for, used to look for

To form the imperfect of -*er* and -*ir* verbs, drop the -*er* and -*ir* and add -*ía, ía, -íamos* and -*ían,* as follows:

*comer* (to eat)

| | |
|---|---|
| yo comía | I was eating, ate, used to eat |
| él/ella/usted comía | he/she was eating, ate, used to eat, you (*for.*) were eating, ate, used to eat |
| nosotros/-as comíamos | we were eating, ate, used to eat |
| ellos/ellas/ustedes comían | they/you (*pl.*) were eating, ate, used to eat |

*salir* (to go out, to leave)

| | |
|---|---|
| yo salía | I was going out, went out, used to go out |
| él/ella/usted salía | he/she was going out, went out, used to go out, you (*for.*) were going out, went out, used to go out |
| nosotros/-as salíamos | we were going out, went out, used to go out |

ellos/ellas/ustedes salían          they/you (*pl.*) were
                                    going out, went out,
                                    used to go out

Note that in all conjugations the first and third person forms are the same. If the meaning is not clear, it's appropriate to use the subject pronouns.

## Verbs that are Irregular in the Imperfect Tense

You'll be relieved to learn that there are only three verbs in Spanish that are irregular in the imperfect tense, *ir, ser* and *ver.* They are as follows:

*ir* (to go)

yo iba                              I was going, went, used
                                    to go

él/ella/usted iba                   he/she was going, went,
                                    used to go, you (*for.*)
                                    were going, went,
                                    used to go

nosotros/-as íbamos                 we were going, went,
                                    used to go

ellos/ellas/ustedes iban            they/you (*pl.*) were
                                    going, went, used
                                    to go

*ser* (to be)

| | |
|---|---|
| yo era | I was, used to be |
| él/ella/usted era | he/she was, used to be, you (*for.*) were, used to be |
| nosotros/-as éramos | we were, used to be |
| ellos/ellas/ustedes eran | they/you (*pl.*) were, used to be |

*ver* (to see)

| | |
|---|---|
| yo veía | I was seeing, saw, used to see |
| él/ella/usted veía | he/she was seeing, saw, used to see, you (*for.*) were seeing, saw, used to see |
| nosotros/-as veíamos | we were seeing, saw, used to see |
| ellos/ellas/ustedes veían | they/you (*pl.*) were seeing, saw, used to see |

## Idioms

The rules of grammar constitute the skeleton of a language, but it's the idioms that flesh it out and give it life. Can you imagine the English language without such idioms as "to be in the same boat," "all of a sudden" and "to have pull"?

So what exactly is an idiom? Put simply, it's an expression, several words long, that is stated differently in different languages. You have already learned a number of idioms in the course of the past lessons so the following is just a small sampling of other common idioms in Spanish. They are followed first with their literal translation and then with examples of their use in sentences:

1. *de golpe* — all of a sudden (literally, "at a blow"):

   *Hablábamos cuando, de golpe, salió del hotel.*
   We were talking when all of a sudden he left the hotel.

2. *cambiar de opinión* — to change one's mind (literally, "to change (of) opinion"):

   *Ibamos a comprar esa casa pero cambiamos de opinión.*
   We were going to buy that house, but we changed our minds.

3. *de todos modos* — at any rate (literally, "of all ways"):

   *De todos modos, voy a vender el carro.*
   At any rate, I'm going to sell the car.

4. *hacer cola* — to stand in line (literally, "to make line"):

   *Para entrar en ese restaurante hay que hacer cola.*
   To go into that restaurant you have to stand in line.

5. *algo es algo* — anything is better than nothing (literally, "something is something"):

   *No me dio mucho dinero, pero algo es algo.*
   He didn't give me much money, but anything is better than nothing.

6. *cumplir años* — to have a birthday (literally, "to fulfill years"):

   *Mi abuelo cumplió años ayer.*
   My grandfather had a birthday yesterday.

7. *¡Cómo no!* — Of course! (literally, "How not?"):

   *¡Cómo no! Tengo muchas ganas de ir con ustedes.*
   Of course! I really want to go with you.

8. *echar al correo* — to mail (literally, "to throw into the mail"):

   *Yo salí para echar la carta al correo.*
   I went out to mail the letter.

9. *entrar por un oído y salir por el otro* — to go in one ear and out the other (literally, "to enter through an ear and leave through another"):

   *Su mamá le dijo la verdad, pero entró por un oído y salió por el otro.*

His mother told him the truth, but it went in one ear and out the other.

10. *tomarle el pelo* — to pull someone's leg (literally, "to take (snatch) someone's hair"):

   *No le creo. Está tomándome el pelo.*
   I don't believe you. You're pulling my leg.

11. *querer decir* — to mean (literally, "to want to say"):

   *Ella no sabe qué quiere decir.*
   She doesn't know what it means.

12. *ser para chuparse los dedos* — to be delicious (literally, "to be for licking the fingers." Does this bring to mind a well-known advertising slogan?):

   *El pollo es delicioso. Es por chuparse los dedos.*
   The chicken is delicious. It's finger-licking good.

Just as in the case of vocabulary, idioms will be assimilated gradually as the learning process continues.

## Exercises

I.  Fill in the blanks with the imperfect tense of the appropriate verbs from the following list:

comer          ser
comprar        servir
ir             tener
pagar

1. Ellos nunca _____ a ese restaurante.

2. Yo siempre _____ mucho a casa de mi abuela.

3. Cuando nosotros _____ en el mercado pagamos muy poco.

4. Mi amigo _____ quince años cuando vivió en Guatemala.

5. El súeter _____ rojo.

6. El mesero _____ el vino cuando llegó mi amigo.

II.  Express the following sentences in Spanish using the imperfect tense:

1. José and Elena used to travel a lot.

2. He was a good doctor.

3. Leonor was dancing and Fernando was singing.

4. I bought meat every day.

5. We used to see him frequently.

6.  Esteban would write postcards to his friends when he was traveling.

7.  Juan's car was black.

III.  Express the following in Spanish:

1.  It's not true that women always change their minds.

2.  All of a sudden the phone rang.

3.  I'm going to buy the gift tomorrow. At any rate, I have to go to the market.

4.  Mr. Olivares had a birthday yesterday. He was 61.

5.  We only ate salad, but anything is better than nothing.

6.  No one likes to stand in line to eat in a restaurant.

7.  Perla went to mail the gift.

8.  When mama tells me something, it goes in one ear and out the other.

9.  It's not true. I believe that Luis is pulling your leg.

10. Of course! You can bring me the chicken. I always order it here.

## Word Study

The phrase "in the morning, afternoon, evening" is expressed in Spanish as *de la mañana, de la tarde, de la noche* when the definite hour is mentioned. The same phrases are translated as *por* or *en la mañana, tarde* or *noche* when no specific time is stated. Examples:

> *El autobús sale a las diez de la mañana.*
> The bus leaves at 10:00 A.M.
>
> *Jaime estudió por la noche ayer.*
> Jaime studied at night yesterday.
>
> *Yo prefiero estudiar en la mañana.*
> I prefer to study in the morning.

## A Few Facts About Central America

Just as in the River Plate region of South America, in many parts of Central America the word *vos* is used as the familiar singular subject pronoun meaning "you." As it is a familiar form, it shouldn't be used by anyone who is not thoroughly knowledgeable about the language and culture of the region. It is, however, useful to recognize it for what it is in order to understand others when they speak.

A helpful soul at the Nicaraguan embassy in Washington maintains that if anyone says *tú* in Nicaragua it's assumed that the person is not from Nicaragua or has not lived there. He adds that *tú* used between Nicaraguans is considered to be "snobby." It's something of a puzzle as to why this language characteristic exists in just two regions of Latin America, regions that are far apart. There are theories, of course, but that's all they are.

The Central American countries are geographically close to one another and thus have much usage in common. However, there are—inevitably—differences as well. Take, for example, the word for "popcorn," which differs so much from country to country throughout Latin America. In parts of Central America it's called *palomitas*; in Panama, however, it's known as *millo.*

Motorists in this region will learn that the correct regional name for "speed bumps" is *túmulos.* However, this annoying artifact of motoring life is also often referred to in a more colloquial, not to mention colorful, way as a *policía acostado,* or a "policeman lying down."

Note: It's not usually possible to rent a car in one country and drive it outside of that country.

As always, each country has its own special food dishes. If you have occasion to move about this area you might like to try the following: In Honduras, *tapado,* a fish, beef or conch stew made with plantain, yucca and other root vegetables in a coconut gravy; in Nicaragua, *nacatemales,* meat tamales topped with salad; in Costa Rica, *gallo pinto,* black beans and rice; in Guatemala, *fiambre,* a dish for special occasions made of several kinds of sausage, bacon, shrimp, sardines and salmon; in El Salvador, *pupusas,* thick fried tortillas filled with ground pork; and in Panama, *carimañolas,* meat, chicken or cheese turnovers.

"Beans," by the way, are *fríjoles* in the area and are pronounced "FREE-hoh-lays." Most English speakers know them as "free-HOH-lays" which is what they're called, for example, in Mexico.

## Vocabulary For Car Travel

Vocabulary related to car travel varies from one Latin American country to another. For example, "tires" are *llantas* in many areas but are *neumáticos* in Chile and Uruguay, *gomas* in Cuba and *cauchos* in Venezuela. "Gas" is generally called *gasolina*, but in Argentina it's called *nafta* and in Chile, *bencina*.

There are also differences in highway signs. Many of the symbols, of course, are recognized internationally and include the following:

| **PROHIBIDO GIRAR A LA IZQUIERDA** | **PROHIBIDO GIRAR A LA DERECHA** | **PROHIBIDO GIRAR EN "U"** | **CEDA EL PASO** |
|---|---|---|---|
| No left turn | No right turn | No U turn | Yield |

However, other signs vary. For example, "Stop" is *Pare* in South America, as seen below. "Stop" in Mexico and Central America is *Alto*. The international symbol for "No Parking" is a circle with a slash through the letter P. In the Spanish-speaking world the slash is through the letter E for *Estacionamiento*, "Parking."

| **PARE** | **PROHIBIDO ESTACIONAR** |
|---|---|
| (*Mex.*) ALTO | No Parking |
| Stop | |

Travelers who plan to drive in Latin American countries should gather maximum information about traffic laws, auto-related vocabulary and highway symbols. U.S. auto clubs are one source of this type of information. Auto rental agencies in the Latin American countries can also provide valuable information.

LESSON

10

# Los Negocios

## Diálogo

*El señor Sergio Flores, comprador de cafés especiales de Miami, Florida, se reune con un agente de ventas de una compañía colombiana de café en Medellín. El agente de ventas, el señor Medina, habla de la cosecha de café de este año:*

**Sr. Medina:** Esta cosecha es pequeña y la calidad es muy alta. Va a traer buen precio en el mercado al por menor.

**Sr. Flores:** Eso sí son buenas noticias. Siempre es un placer poder comprar sus buenos cafés Arábica de altura. ¿Exactamente cuáles eran los resultados de sus pruebas de taza?

**Sr. Medina:** Descubrimos que nuestro café tiene cuerpo mediano y un aroma agradable. Va a ser un buen café de desayuno puesto que tiene una dulzura natural con leche o sin leche.

**Sr. Flores:** Parece un café que le va a gustar a todo el mundo.

**Sr. Medina:** Sí. Ya estamos exportando este café a Europa donde la demanda está creciendo.

**Sr. Flores:** Pues voy a reunirme con su gerente de ventas mañana para finalizar nuestras negociaciones. Por eso le doy las gracias por toda la información.

*El día siguiente el señor Flores se reune con el gerente de ventas, el señor Guillermo Espinoza, en un café popular con los comerciantes de café:*

# Doing Business

## *Dialogue*

*Mr. Sergio Flores, a buyer of specialty coffee from Miami, Florida, is meeting with the sales representative of a Colombian coffee company in Medellín. The sales rep, Mr. Medina, is talking about this year's coffee crop:*

**Mr. Medina:** This crop is small and the quality is very high. It will bring a good price on the retail market.

**Mr. Flores:** That's good news. It's always a pleasure to be able to buy your fine mountain-grown arabica coffees. What exactly were the results of your cuppings?

**Mr. Medina:** We find that our coffee has medium body and a pleasant aroma. It will be a good breakfast coffee as it has a natural sweetness with or without milk.

**Mr. Flores:** It sounds like a coffee that everyone will like.

**Mr. Medina:** Yes. We're already exporting this coffee to Europe where the demand for it is increasing.

**Mr. Flores:** Well, I'll be meeting with your sales manager tomorrow to finalize our negotiations. So I thank you very much for all the information. I imagine that Mr. Espinoza will quote wholesale prices and terms then.

*The next day Mr. Flores meets with their sales manager, Mr. Guillermo Espinoza, in a café popular with coffee dealers:*

**Sr. Espinoza:** Me alegro de verlo otra vez, señor Flores. ¿Cómo andan las cosas en Miami?

**Sr. Flores:** De lo más bien. Andan muy bien los negocios. La gente de la Florida sabe apreciar el café bueno. ¿Y cómo está su familia?

**Sr. Espinoza:** Muy bien, gracias. Usted no puede imaginar como han crecido los niños.

**Sr. Flores:** Bueno, me parece que debemos poner manos a la obra. La calidad de la cosecha de este año de verdad es excelente.

**Sr. Espinoza:** Sí, pero es pequeña.

**Sr. Flores:** Como señaló el señor Medina, eso significa que va a traer un buen precio en el mercado al por menor. Pero ahora nosotros necesitamos hablar de los precios al por mayor.

**Sr. Espinoza:** Por supuesto, van a ser algo más altos que el año pasado también, pero no tanto que ustedes no van a salir muy bien en el mercado al por menor. Aquí están nuestras cotizaciones de precios.

*El señor Flores revisa la lista de precios:*

**Sr. Flores:** Nos parecen aceptables.

**Sr. Espinoza:** Debe saber que hay una cantidad limitada para la exportación. A eso de sesenta a setenta sacos de sesenta kilos de cada tipo.

**Mr. Espinoza:** So nice to see you again, Mr. Flores. How are things in Miami?

**Mr. Flores:** Just fine. Business is very good. The people in Florida know how to appreciate good coffees. And how's your family?

**Mr. Espinoza:** Just fine, thanks. You can't imagine how the children have grown.

**Mr. Flores:** Well, I imagine we should get down to business. The quality of this year's crop is certainly excellent.

**Mr. Espinoza:** Yes, it is, but it's small.

**Mr. Flores:** As Mr. Medina pointed out, that means it's going to bring a good price on the retail market. But now we need to talk about wholesale prices.

**Mr. Espinoza:** Of course they will also be somewhat higher than last year, but not so much that you won't do very well at the retail end. Here are the price quotations.

*Mr. Flores looks over the price list:*

**Mr. Flores:** They're acceptable to us.

**Mr. Espinoza:** You should know that there is a limited amount for export. About 60 to 70 sacks of 60 kilos of each class.

**Sr. Flores:** Compro todo lo que me puede vender, por supuesto.

**Sr. Espinoza:** Aparte del precio los términos del contrato van a ser lo mismo que el año pasado, si ustedes los encuentran satisfactorios.

**Sr. Flores:** No veo ningún problema. Voy a preparar la carta de pedido en seguida. ¿Cuándo puedo esperar su factura comercial?

**Sr. Espinoza:** Voy a mandarla a su hotel mañana. Como siempre, nuestro departamento legal va a encargarse de la licencia de exportación, seguros, etcétera.

**Sr. Flores:** Y nosotros vamos a suministrarles los documentos comerciales, giros bancarios y cartas de crédito en seguida.

**Sr. Espinoza:** El envío de la mercancía debe llegar a Miami dentro de un mes.

*El señor Flores se levanta y estrecha la mano con el señor Espinoza:*

**Sr. Flores:** Como siempre, es un placer trabajar con usted. Saludos a su familia. Lo siento que tengo que salir tan pronto, pero necesito acostarme temprano. Por haber tomado demasiado café anoche, yo no pude pegar un ojo.

**Mr. Flores:** I'll buy all that you can sell me, of course.

**Mr. Espinoza:** Apart from the price, the terms of the contract will be the same as last year, if that is satisfactory with you.

**Mr. Flores:** I don't see any problem. I'll prepare the order letter right away. When can I expect your commercial invoice?

**Mr. Espinoza:** I'm going to send it to your hotel tomorrow. As always, our legal department will take care of the export license, insurance, etc.

**Mr. Flores:** And we'll provide you with the commercial documents, bank drafts and letters of credit.

**Mr. Espinoza:** The shipment of merchandise should arrive in Miami within a month.

*Mr. Flores gets up to leave and shakes hands with Mr. Espinoza:*

**Mr. Flores:** As always, it's a pleasure doing business with you, Mr. Espinoza. My best to your family. Sorry I have to leave so soon, but I need to go to bed early tonight. Because of drinking too much coffee last night, I didn't sleep a wink.

## Vocabulary

| | |
|---|---|
| a eso de | about |
| aceptables | acceptable |
| agente de ventas | sales representative |
| agradable | pleasant |
| al por mayor | wholesale |
| al por menor | retail |
| algo | somewhat |
| alta | high |
| año pasado | last year |
| aparte de | apart from |
| apreciar | to appreciate |
| cafés | coffees |
| calidad | quality |
| cantidad | quantity |
| carta de pedido | order letter |
| cartas de crédito | letters of credit |
| comerciantes de café | coffee dealers |
| ¿cómo andan—? | how are—? |
| compañía | company |
| comprador | buyer |
| con | with |
| contrato | contract |
| cosas | things |
| cosecha | crop |
| cotizaciones de precios | price quotations |
| cuerpo mediano | medium body |
| de altura | mountain-grown |
| de lo más bien | extremely well |
| de verdad | truly |
| debemos | we should |

| demanda | demand |
|---|---|
| demasiado | too much |
| dentro de | within |
| desayuno | breakfast |
| descubrimos | we found |
| dulzura | sweetness |
| en seguida | right away |
| encuentran | you find |
| envío | shipment |
| especiales | specialty |
| esperar | to expect |
| está creciendo | is growing |
| estamos exportando | we're exporting |
| estrecha la mano | shakes hands |
| etcétera | et cetera |
| exactamente | exactly |
| excelente | excellent |
| exportación | export |
| factura comercial | commercial invoice |
| familia | family |
| finalizar | to finalize |
| gente | people |
| gerente de ventas | sales manager |
| giros bancarios | bank drafts |
| haber | to have (helping verb) |
| han crecido | have grown |
| información | information |
| leche | milk |
| limitada | limited |
| lo mismo | the same |
| lo que | that which |
| me alegro | I'm happy |

| | |
|---|---|
| me parece | it seems to me |
| mercancía | merchandise |
| negociaciones | negotiations |
| negocios | business |
| niños | children |
| noticias | news |
| parece | it seems |
| pequeña | small |
| placer | pleasure |
| popular | popular |
| por la mañana | in the morning |
| por supuesto | of course |
| preparar | to prepare |
| pronto | soon |
| pruebas de taza | cuppings, coffee tastings |
| puesto que | since |
| resultados | results |
| revisa | looks over |
| sacos | bags |
| saludos | greetings |
| satisfactorios | satisfactory |
| se reune | meets with |
| señaló | pointed out |
| significa | means |
| siguiente | following |
| sin | without |
| temprano | early |
| términos | terms |
| tipos | types |
| todo el mundo | everybody |
| tomado | drunk (lit.: taken) |

trabajar                          to do business (work)
vender                            to sell


## *Expressions*

Lo siento.                        I'm sorry.
Manos a la obra.                  Let's get down to
                                  business.
No poder pegar un ojo.            Not be able to sleep
                                  a wink.

# Grammar

## *More on the Preterit and the Imperfect*

In general, the preterit and the imperfect tenses can be said to reflect different ways of seeing past actions or conditions.

The preterit describes an action or condition that was completed at a specific time in the past. Certain words or expressions are usually clues that the preterit is called for in a sentence. They include such words and expressions as:

| | |
|---|---|
| ayer | yesterday |
| la semana pasada | last week |
| hace un año | a year ago |
| anoche | last night |

The imperfect reflects an action or condition in progress at some time in the past. The end of the action is of no concern. The following describes the various situations in which the imperfect is called for.

The imperfect is usually used to translate the "was, were" + <u>ing</u> form of the verb in English. Examples:

| | |
|---|---|
| Yo comía. | I was eating. |
| Juan compraba. | Juan was buying. |
| Ellos vivían. | They were living. |

The imperfect is also used to describe a habitual or repeated action in the past. Words and expressions that provide clues that the imperfect is called for include:

| todos los días | every day |
| frecuentemente | frequently |
| cada sábado | every Saturday |
| siempre | always |

Example:

*Mi amigo siempre pagaba la cuenta.*
My friend always paid the bill.

The imperfect tense also conveys the meaning of "used to" as this implies a repeated action. Example:

*Comíamos a la una y media.*
We used to eat at 1:30.

Another clue you should watch for is the word "would" when it is used to imply a repeated action. Example:

*Yo iba al correos los lunes.*
I would go to the post office on Mondays.

When two actions are going on simultaneously in the past and the emphasis is on the action in progress, both verbs will be in the imperfect. Example:

*Ella bailaba y él cantaba.*
She was dancing and he was singing.

However, when an action is in progress in the past and is interrupted by another action, the action in progress is expressed in the imperfect and the interruption is expressed in the preterit. Example:

> *Comíamos cuando llegó Juan.*
> We were eating when Juan arrived.

Description in the past is usually expressed in the imperfect. Example:

> *La casa era blanca.*
> The house was white.

Possession in the past is always expressed in the imperfect. Example:

> *Los señores Vargas tenían un carro azul.*
> Mr. and Mrs. Vargas had a blue car.

Time in the past is always told in the imperfect. Example:

> *Eran las tres de la tarde.*
> It was three o'clock in the afternoon.

In summary, the preterit reflects a simple statement of completed fact in the past. The imperfect, on the other hand, is the tense used to narrate and describe actions and conditions in the past.

### Prepositions

These pesky little words are usually the last forms to be mastered in a foreign language. This is because their use varies so much from one language to another. For example, in English one speaks "to" someone; in Spanish one speaks "with" someone. In English, you get married "to" someone; in Spanish, "with" someone. In English, you "take care of"; in Spanish, the concept of "take care of" is contained in the verb *cuidar* and is not followed by a preposition. There are, in fact, a number of common verbs in which the preposition is implicit. Among them are the following:

| | |
|---|---|
| cuidar | to take care (of) |
| mirar | to look (at) |
| pagar | to pay (for) |
| buscar | to look (for) |
| escuchar | to listen (to) |
| esperar | to wait (for) |

Examples:

*Marta cuida el gato.*
Marta takes care (of) the cat.

*Miran el libro.*
They look (at) the book.

*Yo siempre pago los boletos.*
I always pay (for) the tickets.

*Buscamos buenos restaurantes.*
We look (for) good restaurants.

*Francisco espera el autobús.*
Francisco waits (for) the bus.

In Spanish, the infinitive form of the verb is usually used after a preposition. Examples:

| | |
|---|---|
| sin ir | without going |
| al llegar | upon arriving |
| antes de comprar | before buying |
| después de ver | after seeing |

## Por vs. Para

Two Spanish prepositions that are easily confused are *por* and *para*.

*Para* has the meaning of "for" in the sense of:

1) Destination:
   *Salgo para Buenos Aires mañana.*
   I leave for Buenos Aires tomorrow.

2) Intended for:
   *El dinero es para Alicia.*
   The money is for Alicia.

3) To indicate career goals:
   *Estudio para médico.*
   I'm studying to be a doctor.

4) In the employ of:
   *Veronica y Anita trabajan para una compañía grande.*
   Veronica and Anita work for a large company.

5) For a time in the future:
    *Necesitamos el regalo para el sábado.*
    We need the gift for Saturday.

*Para* has the meaning of "to" or "in order to" when followed by an infinitive:

    *Necesita el dinero para comprar una maleta.*
    He needs the money to buy a suitcase.

The preposition *por* is used to mean "for" in the sense of the following:

1) In exchange for:
    *Emilio compró el suéter por 30 soles.*
    Emilio bought the sweater for 30 soles.

2) For a period of time:
    *Fueron a México por dos semanas.*
    They went to Mexico for two weeks.

*Por* is also used to translate "through," "by" and "per."

    *Ellos quieren viajar por América Central.*
    They want to travel through Central America.

    *El señor García llegó por taxi.*
    Mr. García arrived by taxi.

    *¿Cuánto cuesta por hora?*
    How much does it cost per hour?

There are a number of verbs in Spanish that require the use of a preposition before a direct object when no such preposition is called for in English. For example, in English you say "She entered the room." In Spanish, however, the verb *entrar*, "to enter," must be followed by the preposition *en* before a direct object:

*Ella entró en el cuarto.*
She entered (into) the room.

Another verb like this is *salir*, "to leave." In English you would say, "She left the room." In Spanish, you would say, *Salió del cuarto*, "She left (from) the room."

# Proverbs

Every language has its treasury of folk wisdom in the form of proverbs and Spanish is no exception. Much of their content is not unlike the ideas expressed in English language proverbs. Ultimately, a student of Spanish will want to become acquainted with, at least, the most common of the Spanish proverbs. The following is a small sampling:

*No es oro todo lo que reluce.*
All that glitters is not gold.

—•— ⫷✦⫸ —•—

*Poderoso caballero es Don Dinero.*
(Literally, "Don Dinero is a powerful gentleman," equivalent to "Money makes the world go round.")

—•— ⫷✦⫸ —•—

*Aquellos son ricos, que tienen amigos.*
They are rich, those who have friends.

—•— ⫷✦⫸ —•—

*Más vale tarde que nunca.*
Better late than never.

—•— ⫷✦⫸ —•—

*En boca cerrada no entran moscas.*
Flies don't enter a closed mouth.

—•— ⫷✦⫸ —•—

*Querer es poder.*
(Literally, "To want is to be able to." Equivalent of
"Where there is a will there's a way.")

---

*El que no llora, no mama.*
(Literally, "He who doesn't cry, doesn't suckle.")
It's the squeaking wheel that gets the grease.

---

*Quien con perros se echa, con pulgas se levanta.*
Lie down with dogs; get up with fleas.

---

*Aunque la mona se vista de seda, mona se queda.*
Even if the monkey dresses in silk, she's still a monkey.

---

*Gato con guantes no coge ratones.*
A cat in gloves catches no mice.

Memorize a couple of your favorites. Then introduce them in
your conversations with Spanish-speaking friends and acquain-
tances. They'll be so impressed.

## Exercises

I. The first step in mastering the use of the preterit and imperfect tenses is to recognize when one or the other is called for. In the following exercise, determine which tense in Spanish would correctly translate the verb in English. Example:

Emilio was singing *imperfect* when I entered *preterit* the room.

1. It was _____ six o'clock when John arrived _____.

2. The man was _____ tired and his friend was _____ hungry.

3. Ana read _____ the book last night.

4. He left _____ at two o'clock.

5. What were you doing _____ when José arrived _____?

6. The men were eating _____ while the women were chatting _____

7. He would walk _____ to the store every day.

8. She bought _____ the sweater last week.

9. I was _____ ten years old when my grandmother came _____ to visit.

10. The house we lived in _____ that year was _____ white.

II. At this point it's useful to review the forms of both regular and irregular verbs in the preterit. Fill in the correct preterit forms of the verbs in parentheses:

1. Yo (ir) _____ a La Paz ayer.

2. Nosotros (venir) _____ a la fiesta temprano anoche.

3. Leonor (comprar) _____ los aros en el mercado.

4. Ellas (vivir) _____ en Lima el año pasado.

5. El botones (subir) _____ el equipaje a la habitación.

6. Los señores Peña (llamar) _____ a su vecina.

7. Ella (tener) _____ que salir temprano ayer.

III. It's equally useful to review the forms of both regular and irregular verbs in the imperfect. Fill in the correct imperfect forms of the verbs in parentheses:

1. Ellos (bailar) _____ cuando yo salí.

2. Ellas (comer) _____ frecuentemente en ese hotel.

3. Juanita (ser) _____ muy bonita.

4. Luis (visitar) _____ a su mamá todas las semanas.

5. Los chilenos (jugar) _____ al fútbol cuando llegó Alfredo.

6. Sergio siempre (querer) _____ comprar un carro caro.

7. (Ser) _____ una casa grande.

IV. Express the following in Spanish:

1. The travelers went to Bogotá yesterday.

2. I was talking to (with) my grandfather when my friend arrived.

3. We went to the restaurant with Perla.

4. We were going to the restaurant with Perla when we saw Enrique.

5. The little girl was ten years old when her family came to Costa Rica.

6. They went to the hotel an hour ago.

7. Julia was there yesterday.

8. The coffee buyer paid the bill.

9. Eduardo wrote a book last year.

10. He was writing his book when his sister went to South America.

V. Fill in the blanks with the prepositions *por* and *para,* as appropriate:

1. Mario pasó _____ el hotel.

2. Quiero un boleto _____ ir a Montevideo.

3. El jóven estudia _____ médico.

4. Le doy veinte dólares _____ el suéter.

5. Julio fue _____ la calle Independencia.

6. Necesitamos dinero _____ pagar la cuenta.

7. Esteban compró el regalo _____ su abuela.

8. Roberto necesita los papeles _____ mañana.

9. Fueron a México _____ un mes.

10. Siempre voy al mercado _____ carne.

VI. Fill in the blanks in the following narrative with *por* or *para,* as appropriate:

Salgo _____ México. Voy a viajar _____ avión.

Tengo boleto _____ el jueves. Tuve que pagar

doscientos dólares _____ el boleto. En México,

voy al mercado _____ comprar artesanía. Espero

estar en México _____ dos semanas. Entonces

voy _____ Guatemala _____ una semana más.

VII. Express the following in Spanish:

1. On seeing María, he left.

2. Before eating, they opened the gift.

3. After studying the guidebook, they went to the cathedral.

4. Juan left the room without speaking to (with) Patricia.

5. On presenting the papers to the official, the traveler passed through customs.

## Word Study

There are two words in Spanish that mean "to spend," but they are not interchangeable. *Pasar* means "to spend (time)" whereas *gastar* means "to spend (money)."

Examples:

> *Quiero pasar más tiempo con mi hijo.*
> I want to spend more time with my son.
>
> *Necesito un carro nuevo, pero no quiero gastar el dinero.*
> I need a new car but don't want to spend the money.

## A Few Facts About Colombia

The Colombians have the well-deserved reputation of speaking the best Spanish in Latin America, that is to say, a very standard Spanish, uncorrupted by Americanisms and influences from indigenous languages. It is said that this is true among all classes in Colombia from the lofty aristocracy down to the humble street cleaners. Even the persnickety Spaniards grudgingly admit that Colombians speak "good" Spanish.

As Colombian speech is so known for its classic purity it's no surprise that the country has a long and distinguished history of literary accomplishment. Colombians are very proud, as well they should be, of the intellectual life of their country.

That does not mean that there are no influences from the indigenous culture. An excellent example of this is the name of Colombia's capital, Bogotá. Before the conquest of Colombia by the Spaniards, one of the indigenous tribes, the Chibchas, had established their capital, Bacatá, on the site of modern day Bogotá. The conquerors added to the name of their capital, Christianizing it by calling it Santa Fe (Holy Faith) de Bogotá. In Latin America today, on television, in the news and so forth, it is still often referred to by the full name, Santa Fe de Bogotá.

The coffee business, which is featured in the dialogue for this lesson, is just one of many industries that English-speaking business people deal with throughout Latin America. Each and every one of these industries has its own jargon that simply has to be learned. Fortunately, it's usually a limited number of words as in the example of the coffee trade. Such words as "cuppings," the sampling of the different coffees, known as *pruebas de café* in Spanish, can be added to one's vocabulary with relative ease. The other vocabularies that business people need are common to most, if not all, industries—*cartas de crédito, giros bancarios,* etc.

# A FINAL BIT OF ADVICE

At this point, presumably, you have worked through all the lessons in this book. So now is the time to review what you've studied. With your understanding of many of the basic elements of structure, you will surely find that the dialogues have now become "old friends."

For those students of Spanish who are only seeking survival skills in the language, this introductory level book will provide the essentials for basic communication. Armed with a good dictionary and a relative mastery of these basics, one can communicate amazingly well. It is, of course, repetition and practice that leads to this relative mastery.

For those students who wish to continue their study at an intermediate level there is a considerable amount of structure ahead. Though it is always possible to use the *ir a* + infinitive to express future concepts, there is also a true future tense in Spanish. The conditional tense, which translates the English concept of "would" + infinitive, as in "She said that she would work tomorrow," is another important and much-used tense. A grasp of the perfect tenses, that is, the tenses formed by using the helping verb "have" or "had" with the past participle ("I have eaten there many times," "Maria had been there for an hour when Ernesto arrived."), is also essential to the mastery of the language. And particularly important in Spanish is the subjunctive mood, a mood that exists in English in such contrary-to-fact clauses as "If I <u>were</u> president, I would," etc. However, its use in Spanish is more extensive and calls for substantial study.

In any case, whether the student only seeks basic skills or plans to move on to more advanced study, a firm base in the essentials is indispensable.

Second-language acquisition is work, but well worth the effort. A mother cat had the right idea. She taught her kittens to bark so they could deceive the resident mouse. Her explanation to them was "To survive these days, one should be bilingual."

# KEY TO EXERCISES

**N**ote: Except in the case of exercises that call for filling in blanks with single words or phrases, it's rare for there to be only one possible correct answer. For example, the answer to a question could be affirmative or negative, could include the use of the subject pronoun or not, could respond by using a noun object or a pronoun one, and so forth. This key, of necessity, will provide only one or two of the most likely answers.

## Getting Started—Part 1

I.    1. Buenas tardes.
      2. (Muy) bien.
      3. Bien ¿y usted?
      4. Me llamo _____.
      5. Hasta luego.
      6. Hola. ¿Qué tal?
      7. Muy bien, gracias.

II.   1. Hola. ¿Qué tal?
      2. Hola.
      3. ¿Cómo está usted?
      4. Chau.
      5. Buenas noches.

## Getting Started—Part 2

I.  1. uno  2. seis  3. catorce  4. quince  5. cuatro  6. diez

II.  1. ocho-nueve-cuatro seis-siete-dos-tres
2. seis-ocho-cinco dos-nueve-tres-uno
3. ocho-nueve-tres dos-uno-cinco-cero
4. nueve-cero-cinco seis-uno-tres-cero
5. dos-ocho-cuatro tres-tres-nueve-cero
6. cuatro-cuatro-dos cero-cinco-ocho-nueve

III.  1. cuarenta y seis  2. setenta y tres  3. treinta y dos
4. sesenta y seis  5. noventa y uno  6. cincuenta y cuatro

IV.  1. trescientos sesenta y dos  2. quinientos noventa y seis
3. ciento ochenta y siete  4. novecientos sesenta y tres
5. cuatrocientos diez y seis  6. mil, trescientos ochenta y
siete  7. cinco mil, trescientos setenta y seis  8. tres
millones, novecientos cuarenta y dos, trescientos
cuarenta y cinco  9. veinte y siete millones, quinientos
treinta y uno, seiscientos cuarenta y tres

V.  1. mil novecientos treinta y ocho  2. dos mil  3. mil
ochocientos diez  4. mil novecientos cuarenta  5. mil
setecientos setenta y seis  6. mil cuatrocientos noventa y
dos  7. _____

VI.  1. sexta  2. tercer  3. quinto  4. novena  5. segundo

VII.  1. lunes, el veinte y seis de enero de mil novecientos
cincuenta y dos
2. jueves, el siete de julio de mil ochocientos cincuenta
y seis

3. sábado, el diez y seis de agosto de dos mil uno
4. domingo, el siete de diciembre de mil novecientos
   cuarenta y uno
5. _____

VIII. 1. ocho y diez de la noche  2. seis y quince (cuarto) de
la mañana  3. una de la tarde  4. dos y media  5. cuatro
y veinte y cinco  6. cinco menos quince (cuarto)
7. doce menos veinte

## Lesson 1

I.  l. yo  2. ellas  3. ella  4. nosotros  5. él  6. ustedes
7. usted  8. ellas

II.  1. reclama  2. presentamos  3. llegan  4. buscan
5. espera

III.  1. el hotel  2. la maleta  3. el uso  4. el socio  5. la luz
6. el carro  7. el viaje  8. la inspección  9. el botón
10. el oficial

IV.  1. un hotel  2. una maleta  3. un uso  4. un socio  5. una
luz  6. un carro  7. un viaje  8. una inspección  9. un
botón  10. un oficial

V.  1. los papeles  2. las maletas  3. las salas  4. los carros
5. los socios  6. las remodelaciones  7. los hoteles
8. las luces  9. los hombres  10. los botones

VI. 1. No podemos comer en el hotel.
2. El señor Ortega no es hombre de negocios.
3. El señor Sandoval no es socio del señor Dávila.
4. El señor Ortega no espera al señor Sandoval.
5. El oficial de migración no pone sello en los papeles de viajero.

VII. 1. ¿Presenta el señor Ortega sus papeles en migración?
2. ¿Reclaman ellos el equipaje en la Aduana?
3. ¿Tiene usted sus papeles listos?
4. ¿Llega el señor Ortega al aeropuerto de México?
5. ¿Tiene usted algo que declarar?

(All of the statements in this exercise can also be converted into questions by simply inflecting them as such or by adding ¿verdad? or ¿no? at the end.)

## Lesson 2

I.    1. es  2. somos  3. es  4. es  5. son  6. soy

II.   1. la maleta de Luisa  2. el restaurante del hotel
3. el viaje del señor Ortega  4. el equipaje de Jorge
5. el sistema de la Aduana

III.  1. la habitación bonita  2. el señor amable
3. la cama matrimonial  4. la luz roja
5. un buen hotel *or* un hotel bueno  6. un gran hombre

IV.   1. mi  2. nuestro  3. su  4. su  5. sus

V. 1. subo, como, vivo  2. lee, abre, comprende
3. escriben, suben, venden  4. creemos, abrimos, vivimos
5. beben, comen, reciben

VI. 1. voy  2. vamos  3. van  4. van  5. van  6. va, va

VII. 1. van a comer  2. vamos a pasar  3. va a subir
4. va a reclamar  5. va a presentar

VIII. 1. Sí, hay servicio a la habitación en el hotel.
2. Sí, hay otros servicios en el hotel.
3. No, no hay cama matrimonial en la habitación.
4. Sí, hay restaurante en el aeropuerto.
5. Sí, hay habitaciones dobles en el hotel Meliá Habana.
6. No, no hay que comer en el restaurante del hotel.

## Lesson 3

I. 1. Yo estoy bien.  2. Marta está lista.  3. La carne está
deliciosa hoy.  4. Ellos no están bien.  5. Julio está
cansado.

II. 1. hablando  2. diciendo  3. decidiendo  4. pidiendo
5. viviendo  6. conociendo

III. 1. está sirviendo  2. estoy escribiendo  3. están
comiendo  4. está subiendo  5. estamos tomando

IV. 1. tenemos  2. vengo  3. vienen  4. tiene  5. tengo

V. 1. Ella tiene que comprar vino chileno.
2. Tengo que ir al aeropuerto.

3. ¿Tenemos que comer en ese restaurante?
4. Ramón y Pablo tienen que esperar el postre.
5. Jorge y Luisa tienen que tener una cama matrimonial.
   Son recién casados.

VI.   1. _____   2. _____   3. a  4. a  5. _____

VII.  1. del  2. del  3. de la  4. del  5. al  6. de las

## Lesson 4

I.    1. completamente  2. amablemente  3. lentamente
      4. necesariamente  5. cómodamente

II.   1. Abuelo tiene más hambre que abuela.
      2. Mi yerno tiene veinte y cuatro años y mi hija tiene
         veinte y dos. ¿Quién es mayor?
      3. Tengo mucho dinero, pero usted tiene más que yo.
      4. La bebé es la bebé más bonita de Venezuela.
      5. Juan siempre viene tan tarde como Leonor.
      6. Es la habitación más cómoda del hotel.

III.  1. quiero  2. duerme  3. prefiere  4. pueden  5. quiere
      6. duermen  7. cerrar  8. prefiero

IV.   1. ¿Va a nevar mañana?
      2. ¿Qué tiempo hace en Maracaibo?
      3. Hace mucho calor.
      4. No nieva en Cuba.
      5. No hace (hay) viento hoy.
      6. Hace (hay) sol.

V. 1. Estoy bien, gracias.
2. Caracas está en Venezuela.
3. Cecilia es la mamá de la bebé.
4. Es la una y veinte.
5. Es quince bolívares.
6. Tienen una nieta.

## Lesson 5

I. 1. sirven  2. pide  3. pedir  4. servimos  5. pido
6. pedimos

II. 1. con él  2. conmigo  3. para ella  4. con ellos  5. para
nosotros/-as  6. conmigo

III. 1. Nunca comen en el Restaurante Blanco.
2. No compran ningunos vinos chilenos.
3. No hay nadie en su habitación.
4. No viajan ni a Bolivia ni a Colombia.
5. ¿No necesitan ustedes nada más?

IV. 1. La veo.
2. Las pedimos.
3. El lo tiene.
4. Ella no lo juega.
5. Nosotros la tomamos en el hotel.
6. Quiero verlos. *or* Los quiero ver.

V. 1. Hace  2. dice  3. dar  4. Hace  5. hago  6. dice
7. damos

# Lesson 6

I.    1. estas   2. esos   3. aquellas   4. estos   5. aquellas   6. esos

II.    1. Pongo la maleta en la habitación.
      2. Sí, traigo el libro de guía conmigo.
      3. Sí, sé la fecha de hoy. Hoy es el _____ de
      _____.
      4. Sí, salgo para allá hoy.
      5. Sí, veo la maleta allí. *or* Sí, la veo allí.

III.    1. conocen   2. sabe   3. sé   4. sabe   5. conocemos
      6. conozco

IV.    1. le   2. les   3. nos   4. me   5. les

V.    1. Se lo doy (a ella).
      2. Se lo traigo (a él).
      3. Siempre se la digo (a ella).
      4. Se lo estoy dando (a él).
      5. Nosotros se lo vamos a dar. *or* Nosotros vamos a
      dárselo (a ella).

VI.    1. Me gusta el hotel.
      2. Nos encanta el libro.
      3. Le encanta este país.
      4. ¿Le gusta a Ana esta tienda?
      5. Me encanta el pollo.
      6. ¿Le gusta caminar?

VII.    1. el vino blanco   2. esa maleta verde   3. el taxi amarillo
      4. esta flor rosada   5. el suéter verde

VIII. 1. Mi color favorito es _____.
    2. Mi maleta es _____.
    3. Mi suéter es _____.

## Lesson 7

I. 1. Quiero ésos.
  2. Quiero éste.
  3. Quiero aquélla.
  4. Quiero ése.
  5. Quiero aquéllos.

II. 1. Yo me baño todas las mañanas.
  2. Ella se quita los zapatos.
  3. Juan se acuesta a las once.
  4. Yo me lavo las manos.
  5. Ellos se ponen los suéteres.

III. 1. Traiga (usted) la cuenta, por favor.
  2. Hable (usted) más despacio, por favor.
  3. Vaya (usted) a Migración, por favor.
  4. Salga (usted) del carro, por favor.
  5. Suba (usted) el equipaje, por favor.
  6. Haga (usted) la reservación, por favor.

IV. 1. Traigan (ustedes) la cuenta, por favor.
  2. Hablen (ustedes) más despacio, por favor.
  3. Vayan (ustedes) a Migración, por favor.
  4. Salgan (ustedes) del carro, por favor.
  5. Suban (ustedes) el equipaje, por favor.
  6. Hagan (ustedes) la reservación, por favor.

V. 1. Acabamos de reclamar nuestro equipaje.
2. (Ella) acaba de comprar los aros.
3. Acabo de poner los papeles en la mesa.
4. (Ellos) acaban de traer la maleta a su habitación.
5. Ana acaba de ir al consultorio médico.

## Lesson 8

I. 1. Nosotros comimos en el hotel ayer.
2. Ella estudió esta mañana.
3. Ellos abrieron el regalo el martes.
4. Compré la maleta anoche.
5. Ayer ellos viajaron.

II. 1. dieron 2. vino 3. fuimos 4. fue 5. Fueron 6. dio
7. puso 8. pude 9. dijo 10. estuvieron

III. 1. (Ella) vendió su libro.
2. Alfredo le escribió la tarjeta postal a su hermana.
3. ¿Le vio usted al médico?
4. Fui a Buenos Aires en mayo.
5. (Ellos/as) recibieron el regalo.
6. Comimos el postre delicioso.
7. Bernardo comprendió las direcciones.
8. Mi abuela nos visitó en octubre.
9. Los señores Vásquez vinieron a nuestra casa.
10. Elena le dijo a Ana donde vivimos.

IV. 1. (Ella) pregunta qué hora es.
2. Carlos siempre pide vino chileno.
3. Cuando no sé, le pregunto a Joel.

4. Elena pidió el dinero.
5. Cuando los estudiantes no comprenden algo en la lección, preguntan al profesor.

V.  1. sino  2. pero  3. pero  4. sino  5. sino

## Lesson 9

I.  1. comían  2. iba  3. comprábamos  4. tenía  5. era  6. servía

II.  1. José y Elena viajaban mucho.
2. (El) era buen médico  or  (El) era un médico bueno.
3. Leonor bailaba y Fernando cantaba.
4. (Yo) compraba carne todos los días.
5. Lo veíamos frecuentemente.
6. Esteban les escribía tarjetas postales a sus amigos cuando viajaba.
7. El carro de Juan era negro.

III.  1. No es verdad que las mujeres siempre cambian de opinión.
2. De repente, sonó el teléfono.
3. Voy a comprar el regalo mañana. De todos modos, tengo que ir al mercado.
4. El señor Olivares cumplió años ayer. Tenía sesenta y un años.
5. Solamente comimos ensalada, pero algo es algo.
6. A nadie le gusta hacer cola para comer en un restaurante.
7. Perla fue para echar el regalo al correo.

8. Cuando mamá me dice algo, entra por un oído y
   sale por el otro.
9. No es verdad. Creo que Luis le está tomando el pelo.
10. ¡Cómo no! Usted puede traerme el pollo. Siempre lo
    pido aquí.

## Lesson 10

I.   1. Imp., Pret.  2. Imp., Imp.  3. Pret.  4. Pret.
     5. Imp., Pret.  6. Imp., Imp.  7. Imp.  8. Pret.
     9. Imp., Pret.  10. Pret., Imp.

II.  1. fui  2. venimos  3. compré  4. vivieron  5. subió
     6. llamaron  7. tuvo

III. 1. bailaban  2. comían  3. era  4. visitaba  5. jugaban
     6. quería  7. era

IV.  1.  Los viajeros fueron a Bogotá ayer.
     2.  (Yo) hablaba con mi abuelo cuando llegó mi amigo.
     3.  Fuimos al restaurante con Perla.
     4.  Íbamos al restaurante con Perla cuando vimos a
         Enrique.
     5.  La niña tenía diez años cuando su familia vino a
         Costa Rica.
     6.  Hace una hora que fueron al hotel.
     7.  Julia estuvo allí ayer.
     8.  El comprador de café pagó la cuenta.
     9.  Eduardo escribió un libro el año pasado.
     10. (El) estaba escribiendo su libro cuando su hermana
         fue a la América del Sur.

V.  1. por  2. para  3. para  4. por  5. por  6. para  7. para
    8. para  9. por  10. por

VI. para, por, para, por, para, por, para, por

VII. 1. Al ver a María, (él) salió.
     2. Antes de comer, abrieron el regalo.
     3. Después de estudiar el libro de guía, fueron a la
        catedral.
     4. Juan salió del cuarto sin hablar con Patricia.
     5. Al presentar los papeles al oficial, el viajero pasó por
        la aduana.

# SPANISH-ENGLISH VOCABULARY

| | |
|---|---|
| a | to; at |
| a eso de | about; approximately |
| abrir | to open |
| abuela (f.) | grandmother |
| abuelo (m.) | grandfather |
| acabar | to finish; to end |
| acabar de | to have just |
| a casa | home (after verb of motion) |
| aceite (m.) | oil |
| aceptable | acceptable |
| acercar(se) | to approach |
| acostar(se) (ue) | to go to bed |
| adelante | ahead |
| ¿adónde? | to where? |
| aduana (f.) | customs |
| aeropuerto (m.) | airport |
| afuera | outside |
| agarrar | to seize; to take hold of |
| agencia (f.) | agency |
| agente (m. or f.) | agent |
| argentino | Argentine |
| agradable | pleasant; nice |
| agudo | sharp |
| al | to the |
| al fin | finally |
| al lado | beside |
| al menos | at least |
| al por mayor | wholesale |
| al por menor | retail |

| | |
|---|---|
| alegrar(se) | to be glad |
| algo | something |
| alguien | someone |
| allí | there |
| altar (m.) | altar |
| alto | tall; high; stop! |
| altura (f.) | altitude |
| amable | kind; nice |
| amarillo | yellow |
| amenazado | endangered |
| amiga (f.) | friend |
| amigo (m.) | friend |
| andar | to walk |
| animal (m.) | animal |
| año (m.) | year |
| antes (de) | before |
| anti-inflamatorio | anti-inflammatory |
| aparte de | apart from |
| apreciar | to appreciate |
| aprovechar | to take advantage of |
| apuro (m.) | hurry |
| aquel | that (at a distance) |
| aquél | that one (over there) |
| aquí | here |
| árbol (m.) | tree |
| aros (m. pl.) | earrings (hoops) (S.A.) |
| arqueología (f.) | archaeology |
| artesanía (f.) | crafts |
| así | thus; so |
| ave (f.) | poultry |
| aventura (f.) | adventure |
| avión (m.) | plane |

| | |
|---|---|
| azul | blue |
| bailadora (f.) | dancer |
| bailar | to dance |
| bajar | to go down; to take down |
| bajo | short; low |
| balompié (m.) | soccer (Arg.) |
| bandada (f.) | flock |
| barato | cheap |
| barbería (f.) | barbershop |
| basta de | enough of |
| bastante | enough; rather |
| batería (f.) | battery |
| bebé (f. or m.) | baby |
| bien | well |
| bienvenido | welcome |
| boca (f.) | mouth |
| boleto (m.) | ticket |
| bolívar (m.) | bolivar (Venezuelan unit of currency) |
| boliviano | Bolivian |
| bonito | pretty |
| botella (f.) | bottle |
| botón (m.) | button |
| botones (m.) | bellboy |
| bueno | good |
| buscar | to look for; to seek |
| buzón (m.) | mailbox |
| caballero (m.) | gentleman |
| caer | to fall |
| café (m.) | coffee; café |
| calidad (f.) | quality |
| calle (f.) | street |

| | |
|---|---|
| cama (f.) | bed |
| cámara (f.) | camera |
| cambiar | to change |
| cambio (m.) | change |
| caminar | to walk |
| camino (m.) | road |
| cansado | tired |
| cantar | to sing |
| cantidad (f.) | quantity |
| capital (f.) | capital (city) |
| carne (f.) | meat |
| caro | expensive |
| carro (m.) | car |
| carta (f.) | letter |
| casa (f.) | house |
| casi | almost |
| catedral (f.) | cathedral |
| cebolla (f.) | onion |
| celebración (f.) | celebration |
| cenar | to have dinner |
| cerca | near |
| cerrar (ie) | to close |
| cerveza (f.) | beer |
| chico | small |
| chileno | Chilean |
| choclo (m.) | corn (Chi.) |
| chocolate (m.) | chocolate |
| chupar | to lick |
| ciudad (f.) | city |
| color (m.) | color |
| comenzar (ie) | to begin |
| comer | to eat |

| | |
|---|---|
| comercial | commercial |
| comerciante (*f.* or *m.*) | businessman/woman |
| como | as; like |
| ¿cómo? | how? |
| companía (*f.*) | company; troupe |
| competir (i) | to compete |
| completo | complete |
| comprador (*m.*) | buyer |
| comprar | to buy |
| comprender | to understand |
| con | with |
| conferencia (*f.*) | conference |
| conocer | to know; to be acquainted (with) |
| conseguir (i) | to get; to obtain |
| consejo (*m.*) | advice |
| construir | to construct |
| consultorio (*m.*) | doctor's office |
| contar (ue) | to count; to tell |
| contestar | to answer |
| contrato (*m.*) | contract |
| conversación (*f.*) | conversation |
| convertir (ie) | to convert |
| copa (*f.*) | wine glass |
| correo (*m.*) | mail |
| correos (*m. pl.*) | post office |
| carretera (*f.*) | highway |
| corregir (i) | to correct |
| cosa (*f.*) | thing |
| cosecha (*f.*) | crop |
| costal (*m.*) | bag |
| costar (ue) | to cost |

| | |
|---|---|
| cotización (f.) | quotation |
| crecer | to grow |
| crédito (m.) | credit |
| creer | to believe |
| cruda (f.) | hangover (Mex.) |
| cuadra (f.) | block |
| ¿cuánto? | how much? |
| cuarto (m.) | room; quarter |
| cuenta (f.) | bill; check |
| cuerpo (m.) | body |
| cuidado (m.) | care |
| dar | to give |
| de | of; from; about |
| deber | to owe; should |
| decidir | to decide |
| décimo | tenth |
| decir | to say |
| declarar | to declare |
| dedo (m.) | finger |
| delicioso | delicious |
| demandar | to demand |
| dentro de | within |
| derecha | right |
| desayuno (m.) | breakfast |
| descubrir | to describe |
| desde | from; since |
| después de | after |
| día (m.) | day |
| difícil | difficult |
| dificultad (f.) | difficulty |
| dinero (m.) | money |

| | |
|---|---|
| dirección (f.) | address; direction |
| disfrutar | to enjoy |
| distancia (f.) | distance |
| dólar (m.) | dollar |
| doler (ue) | to hurt |
| dolor (m.) | pain |
| doméstico | domestic |
| ¿dónde? | where? |
| dormir (ue) | to sleep |
| dormir(se) | to go to sleep; to fall asleep |
| dulzura (f.) | sweetness |
| durante | during |
| duro | hard |
| echar(se) | to throw |
| ecología (f.) | ecology |
| ecologista (f. or m.) | ecologist; environmentalist |
| ejercicio (m.) | exercise |
| el | the |
| él | he |
| electrónico | electronic |
| elevador (m.) | elevator |
| elevar | elevate |
| ella | she |
| ellas (f.) | they |
| ellos (m.) | they |
| emocionante | exciting |
| empezar (ie) | to begin |
| empleado (m.) | employee; worker |
| empujar | to push |
| en | in; on |
| en seguida | right away |
| encantar | to enchant; to just love |

| | |
|---|---|
| encontrar(se) (ue) | to meet; to find |
| ensalada (f.) | salad |
| entender (ie) | to understand |
| entonces | then |
| entrada (f.) | entrance |
| entre | between; among |
| enviar | to send |
| envío (m.) | shipment |
| equipaje (m.) | luggage |
| escalera (f.) | stairs |
| escoger | to choose |
| escribir | to write |
| ese | that |
| ése | that one |
| español (m.) | Spanish |
| especial | special |
| especie (f.) | species |
| esperar | to wait; to hope |
| esposa (f.) | wife |
| esposo (m.) | husband |
| esquina (f.) | corner |
| estancia (f.) | stay |
| estar | to be |
| este | this |
| éste | this one |
| estómago (m.) | stomach |
| estrechar | to shake (hands) |
| estudiante (f. or m.) | student |
| estudiar | to study |
| exactamente | exactly |
| examinar | to examine |
| excelente | excellent |

| | |
|---|---|
| experiencia (f.) | experience |
| explicar | to explain |
| exportación (f.) | export |
| exportar | to export |
| factura (f.) | invoice |
| falta (f.) | lack |
| faltar | to lack |
| fauna y flora (f.) | fauna and flora |
| familia (f.) | family |
| farmacia (f.) | pharmacy |
| favorito | favorite |
| fiesta (f.) | party; partying |
| fijo | fixed |
| fin (m.) | end |
| finalizar | to finalize |
| flor (f.) | flower |
| foto (f.) | photograph |
| frenos (m. pl.) | brakes |
| frito | fried |
| función (f.) | performance |
| fútbol (m.) | soccer |
| ganar | to win; to earn |
| ganas (f. pl.) | desire; urge |
| gasolina (f.) | gasoline |
| gasolinera (f.) | gas station |
| gasolinero (m.) | gas station attendant |
| gato (m.) | cat |
| gente (f.) | people |
| gerente de ventas (m.) | sales manager |
| gira (f.) | tour |
| giros bancarios | bank drafts |
| gozar | to enjoy |
| gracias | thanks |

| | |
|---|---|
| grande | large; great |
| gris | gray |
| guacamayo (m.) | macaw |
| guante (m.) | glove |
| guía (f.) | guide |
| gustar | to please; to like |
| gusto (m.) | pleasure |
| habitación (f.) | room |
| hacer | to do; to make |
| hacia | toward |
| hambre (f.) | hunger |
| hasta | until; up to |
| hechizador (m.) | witch doctor |
| helado (m.) | ice cream |
| hermana (f.) | sister |
| hermano (m.) | brother |
| hermoso | beautiful |
| hielo (m.) | ice |
| hija (f.) | daughter |
| hijo (m.) | son |
| hinchado | swollen |
| hombre (m.) | man |
| hora (f.) | hour |
| hotel (m.) | hotel |
| hoy | today |
| huésped (m.) | guest |
| huevo (m.) | egg |
| humor (m.) | humor |
| imaginar | to imagine |
| importante | important |
| impresionante | impressive |
| incluir | to include |

| | |
|---|---|
| información (f.) | information |
| inglés (m.) | English |
| inspección (f.) | inspection |
| instrucción (f.) | instruction |
| intentar | to attempt; to try |
| interés (m.) | interest |
| internacional | international |
| invitar | to invite |
| ir | to go |
| isla (f.) | island |
| izquierda | left |
| joven | young |
| joyería (f.) | jewelry store |
| jubilado | retired |
| juego (m.) | game |
| jugar (ue) | to play (a game) |
| kilómetro (m.) | kilometer |
| la (f.) | the (art.); her, it (pron.) |
| largo | long |
| lavandería (f.) | laundry |
| le | to him; to her; to you |
| leche (f.) | milk |
| lejos | far |
| les | to them; to you (pl.) |
| levantar(se) | to get up |
| ley (f.) | law |
| libro (m.) | book |
| licenciado/a (m., f.) | lawyer (title); holder of university degree |
| limitado | limited |
| lindo | pretty |
| línea (f.) | line |
| listo | ready |

| | |
|---|---|
| llamada (f.) | phone call |
| llamar | to call |
| llanta (f.) | tire |
| llave (f.) | key |
| llegar | to arrive |
| llenar | to fill |
| llevar | to take |
| llorar | to cry |
| llover (ue) | to rain |
| lo que | that which |
| lujo (m.) | luxury |
| luna de miel (f.) | honeymoon |
| luz (f.) | light |
| madre (f.) | mother |
| maleta (f.) | suitcase |
| mamá (f.) | mom |
| mamar | to suckle |
| mañana | morning; tomorrow |
| mandar | to send |
| manejar | to drive |
| mano (f.) | hand |
| manta (f.) | shawl |
| mar (m.) | sea |
| maravilloso | wonderful |
| marcar | to dial |
| más | more |
| matrimonio (m.) | married couple |
| mediano | medium |
| medicamento (m.) | medication |
| médico (m.) | doctor |
| medio | half |
| medio ambiente (m.) | environment |

| | |
|---|---|
| mejor | better |
| menos | less |
| mentir (ie) | to lie |
| menú (*m.*) | menu |
| mercado (*m.*) | market |
| mercancía (*f.*) | merchandise |
| mesa (*f.*) | table |
| mesero (*m.*) | waiter |
| meter | to put |
| mexicano | Mexican |
| mi | my |
| mí | me (object of a *prep.*) |
| miembro (*m.*) | member |
| mientras que | while |
| mientras tanto | meanwhile |
| migración (*f.*) | immigration (lit.: migration) |
| mirar | to look (at) |
| mismo | same |
| mono/a (*m., f.*) | monkey |
| montaña (*f.*) | mountain |
| morir (ue) | to die |
| mosca (*f.*) | fly |
| mostrar (ue) | to show |
| motorista (*f.* or *m.*) | motorist |
| mover (ue) | to move |
| mozo (*m.*) | waiter |
| mucho | much |
| muy | very |
| nacimiento (*m.*) | birth |
| nada | nothing |
| nadie | no one; nobody |
| necesario | necessary |

| | |
|---|---|
| necesitar | to need |
| negociación (f.) | negotiation |
| negocio (m.) | business |
| nervioso | nervous |
| nieta (f.) | granddaughter |
| nieto (m.) | grandson |
| niña (f.) | girl |
| ningún | no |
| niño (m.) | boy |
| nivel (m.) | level |
| noche (f.) | night; evening |
| nombre (m.) | name |
| noticias (f. pl.) | news |
| noveno | ninth |
| nuestro | our |
| nuevo | new |
| o | or |
| ocasión (f.) | occasion |
| octavo | eighth |
| oficial | official |
| ordenar | to order |
| oro (m.) | gold |
| oscuro | dark |
| otra vez | again |
| otro | other |
| padre (m.) | father |
| padres (m. pl.) | parents |
| país (m.) | country |
| palacio (m.) | palace |
| pálido | pale |
| papel (m.) | paper |
| para | for |

| | |
|---|---|
| parar | to stop |
| parecer | to seem |
| parientes (m. pl.) | relatives |
| parte (f.) | part |
| participar | to participate |
| pasado | past |
| pasar | to pass; to spend |
| pasas (f. pl.) | raisins |
| pastel de choclo (m.) | corn casserole (Chi.) |
| pedido (m.) | order |
| pedir (i) | to ask for; to order |
| peluquería (f.) | beauty shop (Cuba) |
| pensar (ie) | to think |
| pequeño | small |
| perder (ie) | to lose |
| pero | but |
| perro (m.) | dog |
| perseguidora | hangover (Pe.) |
| personal | personal |
| pescado (m.) | fish |
| pierna (f.) | leg |
| placer (m.) | pleasure |
| plata (f.) | silver |
| plato fuerte (m.) | main course |
| poco | little (quantity) |
| poder (ue) | to be able; can |
| poderoso | powerful |
| pollo (m.) | chicken |
| poner | to put |
| poner(se) | to put on |
| popular | popular |
| por | for; by; through; per |

| | |
|---|---|
| por si acaso | just in case |
| por supuesto | of course |
| postal | postal |
| postre (*m.*) | dessert |
| precio (*m.*) | price |
| precioso | precious |
| preguntar | to ask (a question) |
| preocupado | worried |
| preocupar(se) | to worry |
| preparado | prepared |
| preparar | to prepare |
| presentar | to present |
| presidencial | presidential |
| prima (*f.*) | cousin |
| primero | first |
| primo (*m.*) | cousin |
| principal | principal |
| probablemente | probably |
| probar (ue) | to try |
| problema (*m.*) | problem |
| pronto | soon |
| próximo | next |
| pruebas de taza (*f.*) | cuppings, coffee tastings |
| público | public |
| pueblo (*m.*) | people |
| puerta (*f.*) | door |
| pues | well (hesitation word) |
| puesto que | since |
| pulga (*f.*) | flea |
| que | who; whom; which (*conj.*); than |
| ¡qué! | how! |
| ¿qué? | what? |
| quedar | to be located |

| | |
|---|---|
| quedar(se) | to stay; to remain |
| querer (ie) | to wish, to want |
| quinto | fifth |
| quiosco (*m.*) | stand, kiosk |
| quitar(se) | to take off |
| quizás | perhaps |
| rápido | rapid |
| ratón (*m.*) | mouse; hangover (*Ven.*) |
| recepción (*f.*) | reception desk |
| receta (*f.*) | prescription |
| recibir | to receive |
| recién casado | newlywed |
| reciente | recent |
| reclamar | to reclaim |
| recomendar (ie) | to recommend |
| recordar (ue) | to remember |
| recuerdo (*m.*) | souvenir |
| regalo (*m.*) | gift |
| región (*f.*) | region |
| registrar(se) | to register |
| regreso (*m.*) | return |
| reír (i) | to laugh |
| relucir | to shine |
| remodelación (*f.*) | remodeling |
| renta (*f.*) | rent |
| rentar | to rent |
| res (*f.*) | beef |
| resaca (*f.*) | hangover (*Bol.*) |
| reservación (*f.*) | reservation |
| resolver (ue) | to resolve |
| restaurante (*m.*) | restaurant |
| resto (*m.*) | rest |

| | |
|---|---|
| resultado (m.) | result |
| reunión (f.) | meeting |
| reunir(se) | to meet |
| revisar | to check |
| rico | rich |
| rojo | red |
| rosado | pink |
| saber | to know (a fact) |
| sacar | to take out |
| sala de espera (f.) | waiting room |
| salir | to leave; to go out |
| salón de belleza (m.) | beauty shop |
| saludo (m.) | greeting |
| satisfactorio | satisfactory |
| seda (f.) | silk |
| seguir (i) | to follow; to continue |
| segundo | second |
| seguramente | surely |
| seguro | secure; sure; certain |
| sello (m.) | stamp |
| semana (f.) | week |
| señalar | to point out |
| sencillamente | simply |
| señor (m.) | Mister |
| señora (f.) | Mrs. |
| señorita (f.) | Miss |
| sentar(se) (ie) | to sit down |
| sentir(se) (ie) | to be sorry |
| séptimo | seventh |
| ser | to be |
| servicio (m.) | service |
| sexto | sixth |

| | if |
| | yes; indeed |
| | always |
| | to mean |
| | following |
| | without |
| .) | system |
| | place |
| | located |
| | on; on top of |
| | niece |
| .) | nephew |
| | partner |
| solamente | only |
| solo | alone |
| sonar (ue) | to ring |
| su | his; her; its; your; their |
| subir | to go up; to take up |
| sueño (m.) | sleepiness; sleep; dream |
| suéter (m.) | sweater |
| sufrir | to suffer |
| sugerir (ie) | to suggest |
| sur (m.) | south |
| sus | your (pl.); their (pl.) |
| tal | such |
| tamaño (m.) | size |
| también | also |
| tan | as; so |
| tanque (m.) | tank |
| tanto | as much |
| tarde | late |
| tarde (f.) | afternoon; evening |

| | |
|---|---|
| tarjeta (f.) | card |
| taxi (m.) | taxi |
| taxista (f. or m.) | taxi driver |
| teléfono (m.) | telephone |
| temprano | early |
| tener | to have (possess) |
| tercero | third |
| terminar | to end; to finish |
| término (m.) | term |
| tía (f.) | aunt |
| tienda (f.) | store |
| tío (m.) | uncle |
| tobillo (m.) | ankle |
| tocar | to touch |
| todavía | still; yet |
| todo | all |
| todo el mundo | everybody; everyone |
| tomar | to take; to eat; to drink |
| torcedura (f.) | sprain |
| trabajar | to work |
| traer | to bring |
| tránsito (m.) | traffic |
| tropezar (ie) | to trip over; to run into |
| túmulo (m.) | speed bump (C.A.) |
| último | last |
| un (m.) | a; an |
| una (f.) | a; an |
| universitario | university |
| uno | one |
| uso (m.) | use |
| usted | you (for.) |
| ustedes | you (pl.) |

| | |
|---|---|
| valer | to be worth |
| varios | various |
| vecino (m.) | neighbor |
| vender | to sell |
| venezolano | Venezuelan |
| venir | to come |
| venta (f.) | sale |
| ver | to see |
| verdad (f.) | truth |
| verdadero | real |
| verde | green |
| viajar | to travel |
| viaje (m.) | trip |
| viajero (m.) | traveler |
| vida (f.) | life |
| visitar | to visit |
| vivir | to live |
| y | and |
| ya | already |
| yo | I |
| zapato (m.) | shoe |

# ENGLISH-SPANISH VOCABULARY

| | |
|---|---|
| a, an | un (*m.*), una (*f.*) |
| about | de; a eso de (approximately) |
| acceptable | aceptable |
| address | dirección (*f.*) |
| adventure | aventura (*f.*) |
| advice | consejo (*m.*) |
| after | después (de) |
| afternoon | tarde (*f.*) |
| again | otra vez |
| agency | agencia (*f.*) |
| agent | agente (*m.* or *f.*) |
| ahead | adelante |
| airport | aeropuerto (*m.*) |
| all | todo |
| almost | casi |
| alone | solo |
| already | ya |
| also | también |
| altar | altar (*m.*) |
| altitude | altura (*f.*) |
| always | siempre |
| among | entre |
| and | y |
| animal | animal (*m.*) |
| ankle | tobillo (*m.*) |
| answer (*v.*) | contestar |
| anti-inflammatory | anti-inflamatorio |
| apart from | aparte de |
| appreciate | apreciar |

| | |
|---|---|
| approach (v.) | acercar(se) |
| archaeology | arqueología (f.) |
| Argentine | argentino |
| arrive | llegar |
| as | como; tan |
| as much | tanto |
| ask (a question) | preguntar |
| ask for | pedir (i) |
| at | a |
| at least | al menos |
| attempt (v.) | intentar |
| aunt | tía (f.) |
| baby | bebé (m. or f.) |
| bad | malo |
| bag | costal (m.) |
| bank drafts | giros bancarios |
| barbershop | barbería (f.) |
| battery | batería (f.) |
| be | ser; estar |
| be able | poder (ue) |
| be acquainted (with) | conocer |
| be glad | alegrar(se) |
| be located | quedar |
| be sorry | sentir(se) (ie) |
| be worth | valer |
| beautiful | hermoso |
| beauty shop | salón de belleza (m.), peluquería (f.) (Cuba) |
| bed | cama (f.) |
| beef | res (f.) |
| beer | cerveza (f.) |
| before | antes (de) |

| | |
|---|---|
| begin | comenzar (ie); empezar (ie) |
| believe | creer |
| bellboy | botones (*m.*) |
| beside | al lado |
| better | mejor |
| between | entre |
| bill | cuenta (*f.*) |
| birth | nacimiento (*m.*) |
| block | cuadra (*f.*) |
| blue | azul |
| body | cuerpo (*m.*) |
| bolivar (Ven. unit of currency) | bolívar (*m.*) |
| Bolivian | boliviano |
| book | libro (*m.*) |
| border | frontera (*f.*) |
| bottle | botella (*f.*) |
| boy | niño (*m.*) |
| brakes | frenos (*m. pl.*) |
| breakfast | desayuno (*m.*) |
| bring | traer |
| brother | hermano (*m.*) |
| business | negocio (*m.*) |
| businessman/woman | comerciante (*m.* or *f.*) |
| but | pero; sino |
| button | botón (*m.*) |
| buy (*v.*) | comprar |
| buyer | comprador (*m.*) |
| by | por |
| café | café |
| call (*v.*) | llamar |
| camera | cámara (*f.*) |
| can (*v.*) | poder (ue) |

| | |
|---|---|
| capital (city) | capital (*f.*) |
| car | carro (*m.*) |
| card | tarjeta (*f.*) |
| care | cuidado (*m.*) |
| cat | gato (*m.*) |
| cathedral | catedral (*f.*) |
| celebration | celebración (*f.*) |
| certain | seguro |
| change (*n.*, *v.*) | cambio (*m.*); cambiar |
| cheap | barato |
| check (*n.*, *v.*) | cuenta (*f.*); revisar |
| chicken | pollo (*m.*) |
| Chilean | chileno |
| chocolate | chocolate (*m.*) |
| choose | escoger |
| city | ciudad (*f.*) |
| clever | listo |
| close | cerrar (ie) |
| coffee | café (*m.*) |
| color | color (*m.*) |
| come | venir |
| commercial | comercial |
| company | compañía (*f.*) |
| compete | competir (i) |
| complete | completo |
| conference | conferencia (*f.*) |
| construct | construir |
| continue | seguir (i) |
| contract | contrato (*m.*) |
| conversation | conversación (*f.*) |
| convert | convertir (i) |
| corn (*Chi.*) | choclo (*m.*) |

| corn casserole (*Chi.*) | pastel de choclo (*m.*) |
|---|---|
| corner | esquina (*f.*) |
| correct (*v.*) | corregir (i) |
| cost (*v.*) | costar (ue) |
| count (*v.*) | contar (ue) |
| country | país (*m.*) |
| cousin | primo (*m.*); prima (*f.*) |
| crafts | artesanía (*f.*) |
| credit | crédito (*m.*) |
| crop | cosecha (*f.*) |
| cry (*v.*) | llorar |
| customs | aduana (*f.*) |
| dance (*n.*, *v.*) | baile (*m.*); bailar |
| dancer | bailadora (*f.*) |
| dark | oscuro |
| daughter | hija (*f.*) |
| day | día (*m.*) |
| decide | decidir |
| declare | declarar |
| delicious | delicioso |
| demand (*v.*) | demandar |
| describe | describir |
| desire | ganas (*f. pl.*) |
| dessert | postre (*m.*) |
| dial (*v.*) | marcar |
| die | morir (ue) |
| difficult | difícil |
| direction | dirección (*f.*) |
| distance | distancia (*f.*) |
| do | hacer |
| doctor | médico, doctor |
| doctor's office | consultorio (*m.*) |

| | |
|---|---|
| dog | perro (*m.*) |
| dollar | dólar (*m.*) |
| domestic | doméstico |
| door | puerta (*f.*) |
| dream | sueño (*m.*) |
| drink | beber, tomar |
| drive (*v.*) | manejar |
| during | durante |
| early | temprano |
| earn | ganar |
| earrings (hoops) (*Arg.*) | aros (*m. pl.*) |
| eat | comer, tomar |
| ecologist | ecologista (*m.* or *f.*) |
| ecology | ecología (*f.*) |
| egg | huevo (*m.*) |
| eighth | octavo |
| electronic | electrónico |
| elevate | elevar |
| elevator | elevador (*m.*), ascensor (*m.*) |
| employee | empleado (*m.*), empleada (*f.*) |
| enchant | encantar |
| end (*n., v.*) | fin (*m.*); terminar |
| endangered | amenazado |
| English | inglés |
| enjoy | gozar |
| enough | bastante |
| enough of | basta de |
| enter | entrar |
| entrance | entrada (*f.*) |
| environment | medio ambiente (*m.*) |
| environmentalist | ecologista (*m.* or *f.*) |
| evening | tarde (*f.*); noche (*f.*) |

| | |
|---|---|
| everybody, everyone | todo el mundo |
| exactly | exactamente |
| examine | examinar |
| excellent | excelente |
| exciting | emocionante |
| exercise | ejercicio (*m.*) |
| expensive | caro |
| experience | experiencia (*f.*) |
| explain | explicar |
| export (*n., v.*) | exportación (*f.*); exportar |
| fall (*v.*) | caer |
| fall asleep | dormir(se) (ue) |
| family | familia (*f.*) |
| far | lejos |
| father | padre (*m.*) |
| favorite | favorito |
| fifth | quinto |
| fill | llenar |
| finalize | finalizar |
| finally | al fin |
| find | encontrar (ue) |
| finger | dedo (*m.*) |
| finish | acabar, terminar |
| first | primero |
| fish | pescado (*m.*) |
| fixed | fijo |
| flea | pulga (*f.*) |
| flock | bandada (*f.*) |
| flora and fauna | fauna y flora (*f.*) |
| flower | flor (*f.*) |
| fly | mosca (*f.*) |
| follow | seguir (i) |

| | |
|---|---|
| following | siguiente |
| for | por, para |
| friend | amigo (*m.*), amiga (*f.*) |
| from | de |
| game | juego (*m.*) |
| gas station | gasolinera (*f.*) |
| gas station attendant | gasolinero (*m.*) |
| gasoline | gasolina (*f.*), nafta (*f.*) (*Arg.*), bencina (*f.*) (*Chi.*) |
| gentleman | señor (*m.*) |
| get | conseguir (i) |
| get dressed | vestir(se) (i) |
| get up | levantar(se) |
| gift | regalo (*m.*) |
| girl | niña (*f.*) |
| give | dar |
| give a bath | bañar |
| glove | guante (*m.*) |
| go | ir |
| go down | bajar |
| go out | salir |
| go to sleep | dormir(se) (ue) |
| go up | subir |
| gold | oro (*m.*) |
| good | bueno |
| go to bed | acostar(se) (ue) |
| granddaughter | nieta (*f.*) |
| grandfather | abuelo (*m.*) |
| grandmother | abuela (*f.*) |
| grandson | nieto (*m.*) |
| gray | gris |
| great | gran |

| | |
|---|---|
| green | verde |
| greeting | saludo |
| grow | crecer |
| guest | huésped (*m.* or *f.*) |
| guide | guía (*m.*) |
| guitar | guitarra (*f.*) |
| half | medio (*m.*) |
| hand | mano (*f.*) |
| hangover | resaca (*f.*) (*Bol.*); cruda (*f.*) |
| | (*Mex.*); perseguidora (*f.*) |
| | (*Pe.*); ratón (*m.*) (*Ven.*) |
| hard | difícil |
| have (possess) | tener |
| have dinner | cenar |
| have just | acabar de |
| he | él |
| her | su |
| here | aquí |
| high | alto |
| highway | carretera (*f.*) |
| his | su |
| home | en casa; a casa (after verb |
| | of motion) |
| Honduran | hondureño |
| honeymoon | luna de miel (*f.*) |
| hope (*v.*) | esperar |
| hotel | hotel (*m.*) |
| hour | hora (*f.*) |
| house | casa (*f.*) |
| how much? | ¿cuánto? |
| how! | ¡qué. . . ! |
| how? | ¿cómo? |

| | |
|---|---|
| humor | humor (*m.*) |
| hunger | hambre (*f.*) |
| hurry | apuro (*m.*) |
| hurt (*v.*) | doler (ue) |
| hurt (oneself) | lastimar(se) |
| husband | esposo (*m.*) |
| I | yo |
| ice | hielo (*m.*) |
| ice cream | helado (*m.*) |
| if | si |
| imagine | imaginar |
| immigration | migración (*f.*) |
| important | importante |
| impressive | impresionante |
| in | en |
| include | incluir |
| indeed | sí |
| information | información (*f.*) |
| insist | insistir |
| inspection | inspección (*f.*) |
| instruction | instrucción (*f.*) |
| interest | interés (*m.*) |
| international | internacional |
| invite | invitar |
| invoice | factura (*f.*) |
| island | isla (*f.*) |
| it | lo (*m.*); la (*f.*) |
| its | su |
| jewelry store | joyería (*f.*) |
| just in case | por si acaso |
| just love | encantar |
| key | llave (*f.*) |

| | |
|---|---|
| kilometer | kilómetro (*m.*) |
| kind | amable |
| kiosk | quiosco (*m.*) |
| know | conocer |
| know (a fact) | saber |
| lack (*n., v.*) | falta (*f.*); faltar |
| large | grande |
| last | último |
| late | tarde |
| laugh (*v.*) | reír(se) |
| laundry | lavandería (*f.*) |
| law | ley (*f.*) |
| lawyer (title) | licenciado (*m.*), licenciada (*f.*) |
| leave | salir |
| left | izquierda |
| leg | pierna (*f.*) |
| less | menos |
| letter | carta (*f.*) |
| level | nivel (*m.*) |
| lick | chupar |
| lie (*v.*) | mentir (ie) |
| life | vida (*f.*) |
| light (*n., adj.*) | luz (*f.*); claro |
| like (*prep., v.*) | como; gustar |
| limited | limitado |
| line | línea |
| listen (to) | escuchar |
| little (quantity) | poco |
| live (*v.*) | vivir |
| long | largo |
| look at | mirar |
| look for | buscar |

| | |
|---|---|
| lose (v.) | perder (ie) |
| low | bajo |
| luggage | equipaje (m.) |
| luxury | lujo (m.) |
| macaw | guacamayo (m.) |
| mail | correo (m.) |
| mailbox | buzón (m.) |
| main course | plato fuerte (m.) |
| make | hacer |
| man | hombre (m.) |
| market | mercado (m.) |
| married couple | matrimonio (m.) |
| me | me; mí |
| mean (v.) | significar |
| meanwhile | mientras tanto |
| meat | carne (f.) |
| medication | medicamento (m.) |
| medium | mediano |
| meet | encontrar (ue); conocer (a person) |
| meeting | reunión (f.) |
| member | miembro (m.) |
| menu | menú (m.) |
| merchandise | mercancía (f.) |
| Mexican | mexicano |
| milk | leche (f.) |
| Miss | señorita (f.) |
| Mister | señor (m.) |
| mom | mamá (f.) |
| money | dinero (m.) |
| monkey (female) | mona (f.) |
| more | más |

| | |
|---|---|
| morning | mañana (f.) |
| mother | madre (f.) |
| motorist | motorista (m. or f.) |
| mountain | montaña (f.) |
| mouse | ratón (m.) |
| mouth | boca (f.) |
| move (v.) | mover (ue) |
| Mrs. | señora (f.) |
| much | mucho |
| my | mi |
| name | nombre (m.) |
| near | cerca |
| necessary | necesario |
| need (v.) | necesitar |
| negotiation | negociación (f.) |
| neighbor | vecina (f.) |
| nephew | sobrino (m.) |
| nervous | nervioso |
| new | nuevo |
| newlywed | recien casado (m.) |
| news | noticias (f. pl.) |
| next | próximo |
| nice | amable; simpático |
| niece | sobrina (f.) |
| night | noche (f.) |
| ninth | noveno |
| no | no |
| nobody, no one | nadie |
| nothing | nada |
| obtain | obtener |
| occasion | ocasión (f.) |
| of | de |

| | |
|---|---|
| of course | por supuesto |
| official (n., adj.) | oficial (m.); oficial |
| oil | aceite (m.) |
| on | en; sobre |
| one | uno |
| onion | cebolla (f.) |
| only | solamente |
| open (v.) | abrir |
| or | o |
| order (n., v.) | pedido (m.); pedir (i); ordenar |
| other | otro |
| our | nuestro (m.), nuestra (f.) |
| outside | afuera |
| owe | deber |
| pain | dolor (m.) |
| palace | palacio (m.) |
| pale | pálido |
| paper | papel (m.) |
| parents | padres (m. pl.) |
| part | parte (f.) |
| participate | participar |
| partner | socio (m.) |
| party, partying | fiesta (f.) |
| pass | pasar |
| past | pasado |
| pay (for) | pagar |
| people | pueblo (m.); gente (f.) |
| per | por |
| performance | función (f.) |
| perhaps | quizás |
| personal | personal |
| pharmacy | farmacia (f.) |

| | |
|---|---|
| phone call | llamada (f.) |
| photograph | foto (f.) |
| pink | rosado |
| place | lugar (m.) |
| plane | avión (m.) |
| play (a game) | jugar (ue) |
| play (an instrument) | tocar |
| pleasant | amable |
| please (v.) | gustar |
| pleasure | placer (m.); gusto (m.) |
| point out | señalar |
| popular | popular |
| post office | casa de correo (f.) |
| postal | postal |
| poultry | ave (m.) |
| powerful | poderoso |
| precious | precioso |
| prefer | preferir (i) |
| prepare | preparar |
| prepared | preparado |
| prescription | receta (f.) |
| present (v.) | presentar |
| presidential | presidencial |
| pretty | bonito, lindo |
| price | precio (m.) |
| principal | principal |
| probably | probablemente |
| problem | problema (m.) |
| public | público |
| push (v.) | empujar |
| put | poner; meter |
| put on | poner(se) |

| | |
|---|---|
| quality | calidad (f.) |
| quantity | cantidad (f.) |
| quarter | cuarto (m.) |
| quotation (price) | cotización (f.) |
| rain | llover (ue) |
| raisins | pasas (f. pl.) |
| rapid | rápido |
| rather | bastante |
| read | leer |
| ready | listo |
| real | verdadero |
| receive | recibir |
| recent | reciente |
| reception desk | recepción (f.) |
| reclaim | reclamar |
| recommend | recomendar (ie) |
| red | rojo |
| region | región (f.) |
| register | registrar(se) |
| relatives | parientes (m. pl.) |
| remain | quedar(se) |
| remember | recordar (ue) |
| remodeling | remodelación (f.) |
| rent (v.) | rentar |
| reservation | reservación (f.) |
| resolve | resolver (ue) |
| rest | resto (m.) |
| restaurant | restaurante (m.) |
| result | resultado (m.) |
| retail | al por menor |
| retired | jubilado |
| return | regreso (m.) |

| | |
|---|---|
| rich | rico |
| right | derecha |
| right away | en seguida |
| ring (v.) | sonar (ue) |
| road | camino (m.) |
| room | cuarto (m.); habitación (f.) |
| run into | encontrar (ue) |
| salad | ensalada (f.) |
| sale | venta (f.) |
| sales manager | gerente de ventas (m.) |
| same | mismo |
| satisfactory | satisfactorio |
| say | decir |
| sea | mar (m.) |
| second | segundo |
| secure | seguro |
| see | ver |
| seek | buscar |
| seem | parecer |
| seize | coger |
| sell | vender |
| send | mandar, enviar |
| serve | servir (i) |
| service | servicio (m.) |
| seventh | séptimo |
| shake (hands) | estrechar (la mano) |
| sharp | agudo |
| shawl | manta (f.) |
| she | ella |
| shine (v.) | relucir |
| shipment | envío (m.) |
| shoe | zapato (m.) |

| short | bajo, corto |
| should | deber |
| show (v.) | mostrar (ue) |
| sick | malo, enfermo |
| silk | seda (f.) |
| silver | plata (f.) |
| simply | sencillamente |
| since | desde; como |
| sing | cantar |
| sister | hermana (f.) |
| sit down | sentar(se) (ie) |
| sixth | sexto |
| size | tamaño (m.) |
| sleep (n., v.) | sueño (m.); dormir (ue) |
| sleepiness | sueño |
| small | pequeño; chico |
| smart | listo |
| smile (v.) | sonreír(se) |
| so | tan |
| soccer | fútbol (m.) balompié (m.) (Arg.) |
| someone | alguien |
| something | algo |
| son | hijo (m.) |
| soon | pronto |
| south | sur (m.) |
| souvenir | recuerdo (m.) |
| Spanish | español |
| speak | hablar |
| special | especial |
| species | especie (f.) |
| speed bumps (C.A.) | túmulos (m. pl.) |
| spend | gastar (money); pasar (time) |

| | |
|---|---|
| sprain | torcedura (f.) |
| stairs | escalera (f.) |
| stamp | sello (m.) |
| stand | quiosco (m.) |
| stay (v.) | quedar(se) |
| still | todavía |
| stomach | estómago (m.) |
| Stop! | ¡Alto! (Mex.); ¡Pare! (L.A.) |
| store | tienda (f.) |
| street | calle (f.) |
| student | estudiante (m. or f.) |
| study (v.) | estudiar |
| such | tal |
| suckle | mamar |
| suffer | sufrir |
| suggest | sugerir (i) |
| suitcase | maleta (f.) |
| sure | seguro |
| surely | seguramente |
| sweater | suéter (m.) |
| sweetness | dulzura (f.) |
| swollen | hinchado |
| system | sistema (m.) |
| table | mesa (f.) |
| take | tomar; llevar |
| take a bath | bañar(se) |
| take advantage of | aprovechar(se) (de) |
| take down | bajar |
| take hold of | coger |
| take off | quitar(se) |
| take out | sacar |
| take up | subir |

| | |
|---|---|
| talk (*v.*) | hablar |
| tall | alto |
| tank | tanque (*m.*) |
| tastings (coffee) | pruebas de taza (*f. pl.*) |
| taxi | taxi (*m.*) |
| taxi driver | taxista (*m.*) |
| telephone | teléfono (*m.*) |
| tell | decir |
| tenth | décimo |
| term | término (*m.*) |
| than | que |
| thanks | gracias (*f. pl.*) |
| that | que; ese (*m.*), esa (*f.*), aquel (*m.*), aquella (*f.*) |
| that one | ése (*m.*), ésa (*f.*), aquél (*m.*), aquélla (*f.*) |
| that which | lo que |
| the | el (*m.*), la (*f.*), los (*m. pl.*), las (*f. pl.*) |
| their | su (*sing.*) sus (*pl.*) |
| then | entonces |
| there | allí |
| there is, there are | hay |
| they | ellos (*m. pl.*), ellas (*f. pl.*) |
| thing | cosa (*f.*) |
| think | pensar (ie) |
| third | tercero |
| this | este (*m.*), esta (*f.*) |
| this one | éste (*m.*), ésta (*f.*) |
| through | por |
| throw | echar(se) |
| thus | así |
| ticket | boleto (*m.*); tique (*m.*) (*Ven.*) |

| | |
|---|---|
| tire | neumático (*Chi., Uru.*); goma (*Cuba*); llanta (*Mex.*); caucho (*Ven.*) |
| tired | cansado |
| to | a |
| to him; to her; to you | le |
| to the | al (contraction of *a* + *el*) |
| to them; to you (*pl.*) | les |
| today | hoy |
| tomorrow | mañana |
| touch (*v.*) | tocar |
| tour | gira (*f.*) |
| toward | hacia |
| to where? | ¿a dónde? |
| traffic | tráfico (*m.*) |
| train | tren (*m.*) |
| travel (*v.*) | viajar |
| tree | árbol (*m.*) |
| trip over | tropezar (ie) (con) |
| troupe | compañía (*f.*) |
| truth | verdad (*f.*) |
| try (*v.*) | intentar; probar (ue) |
| uncle | tío (*m.*) |
| understand | comprender; entender (ie) |
| university | universidad (*f.*) |
| until | hasta |
| up to | hasta |
| urge | ganas (*f. pl.*) |
| use | uso (*m.*) |
| various | varios |
| Venezuelan | venezolano |
| very | muy |

| | |
|---|---|
| visit (*v.*) | visitar |
| wait (*v.*) | esperar |
| waiter | mozo (*m.*); mesero (*m.*) |
| waiting room | sala de espera (*f.*) |
| walk (*v.*) | caminar |
| want (*v.*) | querer (ie) |
| wash (oneself) | lavar(se) |
| week | semana (*f.*) |
| welcome | bienvenido (*m.*) |
| well | bien |
| well (hesitation word) | pues |
| what? | ¿qué? |
| where? | ¿dónde? |
| which | que; ¿qué? |
| while | mientras que |
| who | que; ¿quién? |
| wholesale | al por mayor |
| wife | esposa (*f.*) |
| win (*v.*) | ganar |
| wind | viento (*m.*) |
| wine glass | copa (*f.*) |
| wish (*v.*) | querer (ie) |
| with | con |
| within | dentro de |
| without | sin |
| wonderful | maravilloso |
| work (*v.*) | trabajar |
| worker | empleado (*m.*) |
| worried | preocupado |
| worry (*v.*) | preocupar(se) |
| write | escribir |
| year | año (*m.*) |

| | |
|---|---|
| yellow | amarillo |
| yes | sí |
| yet | todavía |
| you (for.) | usted (*sing.*); ustedes (*pl.*) |
| young | joven |
| your | su (*sing.*); sus (*pl.*) |

# HIPPOCRENE BEGINNER'S SERIES

**BEGINNER'S ALBANIAN**
150 pages • 5 x 7 • 0-7818-0816-2 •
W • $14.95pb • (537)

**ARABIC FOR BEGINNERS**
158 pages • 5½ x 8½ • 0-7818-0841-3 •
W • $11.95pb • (229)

**BEGINNER'S ARMENIAN**
209 pages • 5½ x 8½ • 0-7818-0723-9 •
W • $14.95pb • (226)

**BEGINNER'S ASSYRIAN**
138 pages • 5½ x 8½ • 0-7818-0677-1 •
W • $11.95pb • (763)

**BEGINNER'S BULGARIAN**
207 pages • 5½ x 8½ • 0-7818-0300-4 •
W • $9.95pb • (76)

**BEGINNER'S CHINESE**
173 pages • 5½ x 8½ • 0-7818-0566-X •
W • $14.95pb • (690)

**BEGINNER'S CZECH**
167 pages • 5½ x 8½ • 0-7818-0231-8 •
W • $9.95pb • (74)

**BEGINNER'S DUTCH**
173 pages • 5½ x 8½ • 0-7818-0735-2 •
W • $14.95pb • (248)

**BEGINNER'S ESPERANTO**
342 pages • 5½ x 8½ • 0-7818-0230-X •
W • $14.95pb • (51)

**BEGINNER'S FRENCH**
175 pages • 5½ x 8½ • 0-7818-0863-4 •
W • $14.95pb • (264)

**BEGINNER'S GAELIC**
224 pages • 5½ x 8½ • 0-7818-0726-3 •
W • $14.95pb • (255)

**BEGINNER'S HUNGARIAN**
*Revised with larger type*
166 pages • 5½ x 8½ • 0-7818-0866-9 •
W • $14.95pb • (308)

**BEGINNER'S IRISH**
150 pages • 5½ x 8½ • 0-7818-0784-0 •
W • $14.95pb • (320)

**BEGINNER'S ITALIAN**
192 pages • 5½ x 8½ • 0-7818-0839-1 •
W • $14.95pb • (208)

**BEGINNER'S JAPANESE**
290 pages • 6 x 8 • 0-7818-0234-2 •
W • $11.95pb • (53)

**BEGINNER'S LITHUANIAN**
471 pages • 6 x 9 • 0-7818-0678-X •
W • $19.95pb • (764)

**BEGINNER'S MAORI**
121 pages • 5½ x 8½ • 0-7818-0605-4 •
NA • $8.95pb • (703)

**BEGINNER'S PERSIAN**
288 pages • 5½ x 8½ • 0-7818-0567-8 •
NA • $14.95pb • (696)

**BEGINNER'S POLISH**
118 pages • 5½ x 8½ • 0-7818-0299-7 •
W • $9.95pb • (82)

**BEGINNER'S ROMANIAN**
105 pages • 5½ x 8½ • 0-7818-0208-3 •
W • $7.95pb • (79)

**BEGINNER'S RUSSIAN**
131 pages • 5½ x 8½ • 0-7818-0232-6 •
W • $9.95pb • (61)

**BEGINNER'S SERBO-CROATIAN**
175 pages • 5½ x 8½ • 0-7818-0845-6 •
W • $14.95pb • (138)

**BEGINNER'S SICILIAN**
159 pages • 5½ x 8½ • 0-7818-0640-2 •
W • $11.95pb • (716)

**BEGINNER'S SLOVAK**
207 pages • 5½ x 8½ • 0-7818-0815-4 •
W • $14.95pb • (534)

**BEGINNER'S SWAHILI**
200 pages • 5½ x 8½ • 0-7818-0335-7 •
W • $9.95pb • (52)

**BEGINNER'S TURKISH**
300 pages • 5 x 7½ • 0-7818-0679-8 •
NA • $14.95pb • (765)

**BEGINNER'S UKRAINIAN**
130 pages • 5½ x 8½ • 0-7818-0443-4 •
W • $11.95pb • (88)

**BEGINNER'S VIETNAMESE**
515 pages • 7 x 10 • 0-7818-0411-6 •
W • $19.95pb • (253)

**BEGINNER'S WELSH**
171 pages • 5½ x 8½ • 0-7818-0589-9 •
W • $9.95pb • (712)

Prices subject to change without prior notice. To order **Hippocrene Books**, contact your local bookstore, call (718) 454-2366, visit www.hippocrenebooks.com, or write to: Hippocrene Books, 171 Madison Avenue, New York, NY 10016. Please enclose check or money order adding $5.00 shipping (UPS) for the first book and $.50 for each additional title.